20/20

TWENTY GREAT HOUSES OF THE TWENTIETH CENTURY

JOHN PARDEY

20/20

TWENTY GREAT HOUSES OF THE TWENTIETH CENTURY

LUND HUMPHRIES

CONTENTS

Preface 7

Introduction 11

Schröder House, Utrecht, Netherlands 16
Gerrit Rietveld, 1924

Villa Savoye, Poissy, France 26
Le Corbusier, 1929

Villa Müller, Prague, Czech Republic 36
Adolf Loos, 1930

Tugendhat House, Brno, Czech Republic 46
Mies van der Rohe, 1930

Dalsace House (Maison de Verre), Paris, France 56
Pierre Chareau, 1932

Fallingwater, Bear Run, Philadelphia, USA 66
Frank Lloyd Wright, 1937

Villa Bianca, Seveso, Italy 76
Giuseppe Terragni, 1937

Villa Mairea, Noormarkku, Finland 84
Alvar Aalto, 1939

The Desert House, Palm Springs, California, USA 96
Richard Neutra, 1946

Eames House, Pacific Palisades, California, USA   106
Charles and Ray Eames, 1949

Farnsworth House, Fox River, Illinois, USA   116
Mies van der Rohe, 1951

Utzon House, Hellebæk, Denmark   126
Jørn Utzon, 1952

Niemeyer House (Casa das Canoas), Rio de Janeiro, Brazil   136
Oscar Niemeyer, 1953

Maisons Jaoul, Paris, France   144
Le Corbusier, 1955

Stahl House (Case Study House 22), Los Angeles, California, USA   154
Pierre Koenig, 1960

Gwathmey House, Amagansett, New York, USA   164
Charles Gwathmey, 1965

Fisher House, Hatboro, Philadelphia, USA   172
Louis Kahn, 1967

San Cristóbal, Mexico City, Mexico   182
Luis Barragán, 1968

Can Lis, Porto Petro, Majorca   192
Jørn Utzon, 1972

Marie Short House, Kempsey, Australia   204
Glenn Murcutt, 1975

Acknowledgements   216
Select Bibliography   217
Image Credits   219
Index   220

PREFACE

THE HOUSE IS CENTRAL to all human life for it is the container for our lives. We all have strong attachments to our home. In the deepest past, houses were built from available materials to provide shelter. They were not designed; they were simply built. But as cultures developed, buildings began to be planned and so they were founded on an idea, and architecture happens when buildings embody a concept.

The Greek and Roman civilisations created rules to guide how buildings should be designed and this gave rise to 'classical' architecture, the principles of which were to ripple across the subsequent millennia. By the 19th century, developed countries indulged in either the classical or the gothic means of expression, but these were limited by the methods of construction. Essentially, most buildings were made by stacking heavy materials on top of each other – brick, stone, rubble – and architects learnt how to stretch these materials to incredible means, as the domes of numerous cathedrals testify. Timber was also used but lacked longevity and was strictly limited structurally. This was to change with the Industrial Revolution and the manufacture of cast iron, then steel, concrete and glass. The Crystal Palace built in Hyde Park in 1851 for the Great Exhibition may not have been the first building to use cast iron and glass, but it was to be the most revolutionary demonstration of these new materials. Built in a machine-made, modular construction, it not only introduced an implausibly slender vertical structure and large spans that leapt across the sky but brought about a new conception of space that was diaphanous, filigree and almost immaterial.

Exactly one hundred years later, the German architect Mies van der Rohe was to build a house on the banks of a river in Illinois, USA, that reinvented the house as a similarly diaphanous glass-walled container. With steel and reinforced concrete, architects in the 20th century were freed from gravity and, with the house as a kind of laboratory for their ideas, architecture was transformed.

Alongside the new materials and structural possibilities, the 20th century also saw an explosion in ideas – in science, physics, literature, poetry, medicine, philosophy – and this was reflected in the world of art. As artists explored representation, free from conventions, Impressionism quickly led to abstraction, and these ideas permeated architecture. It was no longer enough to build using past conventions and, with new materials giving freedom, architects used the house as a vehicle not just to provide space for living, but also to demonstrate and test ideas – about how we build, about abstract concepts, about man's relationship to nature, about place, history and culture.

The 20 houses featured in this book all succeeded in leading the world of ideas. Each was groundbreaking in its day and each embodies a philosophy. Some of these houses have flaws, and some failed to please their clients. Sometimes the bigger the ideas they pursued, the less successful they were to live in. But they all were the first of their type and they all influenced architects around the world, and still do. They are all beautiful, inspiring and profound.

There are plenty of books and monographs on the houses featured here so, while I have attempted to make everything as accurate as possible, I have not attempted to write an academic study. I have described the houses from my visits to them, along with studying their plans, rather than from secondary sources.

From the outset, I was as fascinated by the architects who devised these marvellous works as I was by their creations and, although I have had the great pleasure to meet two of them (Utzon and Murcutt), I knew little about the rest. I have therefore read everything I could lay my hands on to find out as much as I could about their biographies. I admit that I have also trawled the Internet for some further detail but I have treated this with great caution (I do hope the story reported in the American press that some of Barragán's ashes ended up as a diamond is in fact true).

I have also wondered what kind of people commissioned these houses. It is easy when the architect is building for himself, such as the Eames, Utzon and Niemeyer homes, but what brave souls allowed their architect to build such wonderful, often on the edge, houses? Some were built for wealthy entrepreneurs, some for middle-class professionals, a few for friends or ordinary people who wanted something different, and even one for the architect's trusting parents. Each house was the product of both the architect and the client (or the architect

PREFACE

and their family), and from my own work I have learnt that a good house has to come out of a trust between the two parties. If this is lacking or breaks down, unless you are as stubbornly gifted as Mies van der Rohe, the result will always be bad. So, the client's lives are intrinsically part of the story I have tried to tell. How enlightened Edgar Kaufmann was to create two of the greatest houses ever built with two of the greatest architects of the 20th century. Whether he was a good man or not, I am not so sure, but we all owe him a great debt for this.

The fate of these houses is perhaps predictable; eight are already state-owned and act as museums, open to the public, and, in time, the rest will surely follow. At least, unlike great works of art, they cannot be bought and sold for sums the size of a small country's GDP. These houses have to remain rooted to their place, left out in the rain, for architecture is little without context. Visiting them will give future generations endless wonder and joy and that is something both architect and client would surely be happy with.

INTRODUCTION

ON 19 JUNE 2015, ABOUT 90 minutes south of Pittsburgh on PA Route 381 between the villages of Bear Run and Ohiopyle, a sign carved in stone announced that the next turn was 'Fallingwater'. Driving through woodland, a couple of pay booths appeared and, after handing over tickets, we came to an enormous, well-concealed car park. From there, it was a short walk through the woods to a large timber-built visitor centre with the usual cafe, toilets and shop, where we were allotted a time-slot for 'the tour'. I was to be one of 167,270 visitors that year to 'America's most famous house'. It was of course disappointing to be corralled into a small party and have a young but enthusiastic student talk us around the building on a carefully choreographed exploration.

    Approaching Fallingwater and having read dozens of books on the house, it was much as I had expected – assertive, layered and beautiful, hovering above a river – only the peculiar slightly fleshy colour of the balconies surprised. Until, that was, we were taken around the back of the house and told to enter the 'front' door. We stooped into a low, dark, cave-like space and climbed a half flight of stairs that led into the main living space, where the disappointment was instant. The room was cluttered, low and dark, with a glaring strip of light from the windows. The floors were heavy and uneven. The built-in seating around the room all faced away from the view out to the trees – and where was that waterfall I could hear? Now, I knew that in the history of modern architecture that this was an important house and it certainly delighted upon arrival – as it did again later when we were allowed to walk to the 'Viewing Point' to see the full power of its form, clinging to the wooded hillside, suspended above the water – yet once within, it failed utterly to live up to its hype. Every single account I had read praised the house inside and out; every detail, every ledge and every piece of carefully chosen furniture lauded. I felt somewhat betrayed by all I had read.

I decided that night, during a fierce thunderstorm that kept me awake for hours, to write an account of how this architect, from another country and from another era, saw this flawed work of genius – not only how the house came to be, but the story of the client, the architect and the influence of the house in its time and beyond. This led me to think about other great houses and how they related to Frank Lloyd Wright's undoubted masterpiece – not to rank them into some kind of architectural top ten, although I did settle on 20 – but, by looking at them chronologically, to tell a story about the developments in architecture during the tumultuous 20th century; surely the most turbulent, transformative and creative period in human history. This was an era that followed the Industrial Revolution and saw the first global wars and mechanised destruction. It also produced more technological and technical development than any other since the dawn of man and, with the world's population exploding, transport and the freedom to travel became the norm.

My top 20 will not necessarily be another's top 20, but I had a few rules when making my selection: the houses had to have been in some way original and to have moved architecture forward; they therefore had to be influential; they had to be interesting; and I had to want to visit and write about them. There were, of course, difficult decisions to be made in arriving at the 20 houses. Should Wright's Robie House of 1909, Adolf Loos's Steiner House of 1910 or Josef Hoffmann's Palais Stoclet of 1911 be included? The Robie house was original, but somehow seemed rooted in the previous century; the Steiner House anticipated rationalism, but Loos had yet to work out his *Raumplan* concept; and the Stoclet is definitely a complete work of art, but architecturally remains dated, referring to the Secession style.

Then there was the choice of which Loos building to include – the Moller House in Vienna of 1928, or the Müller House in Prague of 1930. Both are world-class buildings and, while I perhaps prefer the former house, as the last significant building designed by Loos and the most comprehensive demonstration of the *Raumplan*, the Müller House won through. And should philosopher Ludwig Wittgenstein's masterful house for his sister in Vienna of 1928 be included? While a wonderful demonstration of the intellect and paradigm of proportion, the house essentially takes its concepts from his close friend Loos's work.

INTRODUCTION

Another struggle was why I should include Charles Gwathmey's house and not Richard Meier's Smith House? While both architects were mining the Corbusian white villas of the 1920s and 1930s, and the Smith House of 1965 is a most accomplished and singular vision, it is the house Gwathmey designed and built that year for his parents that had the most influence. As a smaller house, it condensed the Corbusian ideas and, with an added level of abstraction, it created something original. Meier's work across a long career has been incredibly consistent but has never strayed far from the Corbusian antecedent.

Dates of each house presented another problem. Despite extensive research on each, published dates rarely matched. As an example, the Villa Savoye is widely dated as 1929. Written records show that Corbusier started work on the design in September 1928 (although the Foundation Le Corbusier say it was 'formulated in 1927') and the house took a year to complete, so was completed in late 1929. It was not however occupied by the Savoyes until 1930. So, should a building be dated by the year it was conceived by the architect, or by the year it was completed, or by the year it was occupied? For me, like having a child, it is the date the house appeared fully formed – completed – that won the day.

No houses are included from the first, or last, quarter of the century, while the period 1924 to 1975 was fecund and amazingly creative. Nine of the selection were produced within ten years prior to the Second World War. The influence of Corbusier across the 20th century was profound, like Picasso in the world of art. Perhaps only Wright could truly claim some immunity, but even then, in trying to counter European trends, his output ends up working alongside them. This influence came about by Corbusier's self-belief and his ability to codify his theories, with his *Vers une architecture* (*Towards an Architecture*) becoming the most influential treatise since Andrea Palladio's *Quattro libri dell'architettura* (*The Four Books of Architecture*), written some 350 years previously. But visit any big city in the world today and it is the work of Mies van der Rohe that has probably left the greatest impression, albeit in diminished form, with every steel and glass tower, now ubiquitous from London to Jakarta. Less indeed proved to be more.

While the main narrative across the century was Corbusian, the truly great architects took their own path in developing this into a unique form. Gerrit Rietveld somehow took the idea of the universal language of the Dutch De Stijl movement to create a house that was more a three-dimensional work of art. Loos ran counter to the Corbusian free plan with his ideas of *Raumplan*, an interlocking of volumes within the shell of the house, each sized according to need. Mies took a classical architecture and stripped it back to the essence.

He ennobled the structural frame and embraced space with glass. His love of craft and precious natural materials ensured his work was never sterile but achieved a sense of spirituality. Pierre Chareau went from furniture design to creating a house that was almost a giant piece of furniture, and in doing so developed an enormously sophisticated machine for living. Alvar Aalto began to give the International Style a more natural and humane language and Jørn Utzon took this further to create what is now known as Scandinavian modernism: brick, tile, timber and pitched roofs replacing white render and flat roofs. Giuseppe Terragni fused a purely Corbusian language with a classical tradition and injected an abstraction that years later again surface in the work of the New York Five. Luis Barragán took the simplicity of the International Style and infused it with extraordinary colour planes, to breathe an exotic and sensuous dimension to his spaces. Oscar Niemeyer took the more voluptuous forms of Corbusier and developed his free-form modernism into a paean to the natural beauty of the female form. Louis Kahn turned the world of Corbusier's free plan on its head, returning to the Roman precedents and the notion of 'rooms' – discrete spaces – while Corbusier abandoned his own rules in returning to ancient prototypes and natural materials. Richard Neutra, Pierre Koenig and Charles and Ray Eames fused Mies's simplicity with a Wrightian extension of indoor and outdoor spaces – both in turn looking back across the Pacific to traditional Japanese architecture. And Glenn Murcutt did things his own way: from a Miesian beginning, he developed his language by looking back at Aboriginal art, and then the architecture of early settlers, to create a uniquely Australian modernism.

From the perspective of the second decade of the 21st century, it is already more than 40 years since Murcutt's Marie Short House was built and, to my mind, no other house since has matched its attainment. In the wider spectrum of architecture, there have been many 'isms' – postmodernism, structural expressionism ('high-tech'), neo-futurism, deconstructivism – but no *zeitgeist*, no overriding movement, save perhaps the tendency for iconic buildings, or the crumpled metal forms of Frank Gehry, the slinky, sea anemones of Zaha Hadid or the rather knowing, clever boxes of Herzog and de Meuron. There have, of course, been some very beautiful houses, with the Koshino House in Japan by Tadao Ando from 1982, the Villa Busk in Norway by Sverre Fehn from 1990 and the Villa dall'Ava in France by OMA/ Rem Koolhaas from 1991 all standing out. In the 21st century, perhaps Álvaro Siza's jagged house on Majorca from 2008 and Patkau's stealth-like, angular Tula House from 2015 perched atop an enormous boulder overlooking the ocean in British Columbia will be the first on any top 20 list, with their entirely original and masterful designs.

The average age of the architects of the 20 houses – all men, save Bernice (Ray) Eames – when they produced their masterpieces was 49, exactly the age that Louis Kahn's career really began, so proving that tenacity and perhaps a little grey (or no) hair are key qualities in being a great architect. And how incredible it is to realise that three of the architects of these great houses were essentially furniture designers: Rietveld, Chareau and the Eameses.

Perhaps the one thing that unifies these houses is the way they all attempt to unite inside and outside space. Full-height glazed screens, windows that lower into the floor, windows that frame great slices of nature, outdoor terraces that celebrate the horizon and the sky – only Chareau's Dalsace House fails to do this literally, yet his translucent glazed screen brings the outside light into more focus within than any other.

So, which is the greatest house? Corbusier's Villa Savoye has to be the seminal house of the 20th century. It was the culmination, and the end, of his development of the Five Points that influenced not just his generation but continues to influence architects today. For him, the dream of a perfect Purist edifice was broken as the roof leaked, his clients complained and the rendered surfaces stained and cracked. It remains, like Picasso's *Guernica*, the high point in artistic achievement in architecture in the 20th century. For me, however, it is Neutra's Desert House that offers the most perfect example of a 20th-century house. It utilised technologies of the day to create an elegant, open structure that connected inside and outside in a consummate way. It avoided a particular 'style' by blending International Style sensibilities with natural materials and landscape.

After a life devoted to architecture, it has been a revelation and a joy to visit these houses, spread across the world.

SCHRÖDER HOUSE, UTRECHT, NETHERLANDS

Gerrit Rietveld, 1924

OF ALL THE GREAT HOUSES of the 20th century, the Schröder house is surely the first and the most radical. While it sits at the end of a normal apartment block and is broadly a house-sized 'box', everything else sets it apart from what is expected of a house. It has become the architectural standard bearer for the Dutch De Stijl (The Style) movement that was founded in 1917. And this all came from a furniture-maker turned architect.

Gerrit Thomas Rietveld was born and lived above his father Johannes's furniture workshop in Utrecht. He was one of six children of strict members of the Dutch Reformed Church – his father was a deacon – so the Calvinist doctrine was the guiding principle of his upbringing. Leaving school at 11, but with a talent for drawing, he went to work in his father's workshop. In 1904, aged 16, he enrolled for evening classes in Industrial Arts at the Utrecht Museum of Applied Arts to study under the architect P.J.C. Klaarhamer. Four years later, he received a prize as a highly promising student. By the age of 23 he had married Vrouwgien Hadders, a woman five years his senior, and within two years he had set up his own workshop. Like his father before him, he had six children and enjoyed a happy marriage within the confines of his religious beliefs. This was set to change dramatically when he met the pharmacist Truus Schröder-Schräder in 1921, ten years into his marriage.

In 1913, with Europe on the brink of the first global war, the young architect and communist (despite being married to a member of the Dutch royal family) Robert van't Hoff travelled to America after having seen the Wasmuth Edition of Frank Lloyd Wright's work that had been published in Germany in 1911. Spending time in Wright's office in 1913–14, he returned to Holland with Wright's message. By late 1914, he had built a small house for J.N. Verloop in the village of Huis ter Heide near Utrecht and, wanting furniture to suit the house, approached Rietveld and asked him to make some copies of Wright's furniture, together with new pieces in a similar style. Shortly afterwards, van't Hoff gained the commission for a larger house nearby for the businessman A.B. Henny. He used this project to build a distinctly Wrightian house and in the process created the first reinforced concrete-framed house in Europe (not without some setbacks, as the first casting collapsed, but lessons were learnt and the subsequent construction held up). He again asked Rietveld to provide new furniture pieces, among which was a reclining chair, built in De Stijl mode with simple, rectilinear timber sections and

LEFT:
Gerrit Rietveld in
c.1940

RIGHT:
Robert van't Hoff's
Villa Henny, Huis ter
Heide, 1916

plywood planes. Later, van't Hoff introduced Rietveld to his circle of friends who were to be co-signatories and founders of De Stijl and he and the painter Bart van der Leck suggested that Rietveld's chair be painted in primary colours in accordance with their credo. And so, the famous Red-Blue Chair was born.

The Red-Blue Chair is best seen as a treatise on the nature of space. It simultaneously captures and defines space with its 13 wooden sections that touch but do not intersect. Two flat armrests and two plywood planes are set within the framework diagonally to provide seat and backrest. Adding colour to the elements gave weight to the idea that the chair was at the nexus of an almost infinite spatial continuum. The yellow ends to the sections emphasise the reading that they have been severed from an endless extension into the space beyond.

A close group of painters, sculptors, architects and writers came together in the summer of 1917 to publish a new monthly journal, *De Stijl*, founded and edited by Theo van Doesburg, who was to continue as its guiding spirit until his early death in 1931. Their aim was a new kind of visual art: Neoplasticism, or *de nieuwe beelding*, which was to become one of the most revolutionary arts movements of the 20th century. It spread across Europe with its rigorous principle of harmony above individualism. The first manifesto was signed by the painters van Doesburg, Piet Mondrian and Vilmos Huszár, the architects van't Hoff and Jan Wils, along with the poet Antony Kok and the sculptor Georges Vantongerloo. Their shared credo was the complete elimination of any reference to objects in nature, aiming towards the principle of absolute abstraction. The means of expression was condensed to horizontal and vertical lines, and to the three primary colours – red, yellow and blue – and the three non-colours – black, white and grey. In their first manifesto, they declared that:

ABOVE:
Interior view of Schröder House

LEFT:
Gerrit Rietveld's Red-Blue Chair

RIGHT:
Gerrit Rietveld with Truus Schröder in c.1960

SCHRÖDER HOUSE, UTRECHT, NETHERLANDS

The War is destroying the old world with its contents:
individual domination in every state.
The new art has brought forward what the new
Consciousness of time contains:
A balance between the universal and the individual.

Founded during the First World War, in a neutral country, they saw Europe around them in utter chaos and yearned for a future harmony that they believed could only be achieved with the precision that abstraction offered, as in music. Perhaps echoing the Dutch national character of Calvinism (whose first act in the 16th century was the destruction of the images of worship in their churches), De Stijl aimed to ensure harmony through use of a strictly limited palette, perhaps encapsulated in the Dutch word *Schoon* which means clean and pure, as well as beautiful. Holland itself, of course, was an abstract construct, a man-made countryside, divided up by geometry and precision to deal with a land below sea level.

With the Red-Blue Chair, Rietveld became something of an overnight success and, joining the De Stijl group in 1918, became a standard bearer until Mondrian took over with his beguiling, Calvinist geometric paintings. For the next five years, Rietveld continued making furniture, as well as beginning to make alterations to several shops in Utrecht. He also managed the alterations to Truus Schröder's private room in her mansion in Biltstraat. After her husband's early death, Truus approached Rietveld about building a small house for her to live in until her children had finished primary school, when she intended to move to Amsterdam to live near her sister. Together they found a small site at the end of Prins Hendriklaan, on the outskirts of Utrecht. They also became lovers.

Truus was demanding in her ambitions for this modest house and pushed Rietveld to be innovative – wanting a house that liberated her from the past, and that was flexible and open. Rietveld later claimed, 'And when I got the chance to make a house based on the same principles as that chair, I seized it eagerly'.

Working with Truus was to be a true collaboration and produced not only Rietveld's masterpiece, but also his first completed building. She was not only a very independent modern woman, but a widow in her mid-thirties with three children who

21

had struggled in her rather unhappy marriage to an older man of some social status (he had been a wealthy lawyer). She wanted the house to be a demonstration of how living in the 20th century could be different from the 19th-century lifestyles that still persisted. She later recalled that, 'Once I baby-sat for a friend of mine who lived in a large, empty attic space. I sat there that evening and imagined what it would be like to live somewhere like that. I think for me that was the beginning of thinking about this sort of lifestyle.'

Rietveld approached the design of the house as he had the Red-Blue Chair, with space as the nexus within the building and its continuation beyond the shell. With a plan of only 7 x 10 m (23 x 33 ft) and set on two floors, the house is remarkably small. Truus wanted to live at first-floor level to enjoy the views across to open countryside so, to sidestep the building codes of the day, the ground floor was designed with conventional rooms and a built-in garage (although she never owned a car), while the radical and largely open-plan first floor was simply labelled as an 'attic' on plans submitted to the local authority. A staircase and a small chimney stack sit in the centre of the plan and on the ground floor these are wrapped by three bedrooms, the garage (later to be converted to a studio) and a bathroom. The brightly painted entrance hall, with blue floor and ceiling,

TOP:
Gerrit Rietveld's Kröller-Müller Sculpture Pavilion, Otterlo, 1955

BOTTOM:
The east facade of Schröder House

Plan of
Schröder House

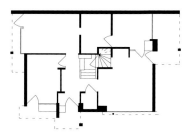
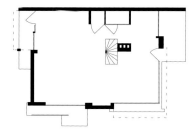

Ground floor · First floor

has a short flight of four steps where a yellow sliding screen reveals a tightly winding black staircase. This wraps itself around a vertical timber post painted bright red, with a black-painted tubular metal handrail attached to it – possibly the only vertical handrail in the 20th century, and a sign of what was to come on the floor above.

The first floor – along with the exterior of the house – is what makes the house innovative and progressive. It is the first truly open-plan domestic space in architecture, although this was partially realised by Corbusier's Dom-ino and Maison Citrohan designs that began to find form with his early villas in 1922 and 1923. There are two plans for the first floor; one closed and the other open. This was made possible by a series of sliding screens that transformed the open floor into a series of smaller spaces – rooms. Apart from a small toilet cubicle, the screens slide out to enclose four sleeping spaces and a bathroom. At the heart of the house, the staircase is crowned by a glazed lantern that floods the interior with daylight. It is joined to a chimney to create a core around which the transformation of the space takes place. The enclosed sleeping spaces each had a divan bed, a washbasin and cooking facilities – symbols of the daily rituals of life – as if flexible monastic cells.

Once opened, with the screens withdrawn, the space had unrestricted views through windows on three sides. Although open, the space was delineated by a geometric pattern of coloured panels on the floor, in black, grey, white and red, while above, painted sliding screen tracks create lines in red and yellow. It also brings the traditional Japanese tatami mat interiors to mind. The house at this point became a moveable background to life.

The north-east point is given over to windows that dissolve the corner when the casements are opened. This was the main social area where Truus placed her dining table. Rietveld built in cupboards, shelves, storage units and beds and these were supplemented with his De Stijl furniture. The overall effect is startling, like being within a three-dimensional Mondrian painting. This continues seamlessly to the outside where each elevation appears as a composition of autonomous planes in white, light and dark grey. These lie one on top of another and refuse to go around a corner. Rather, they overlap to drive home their independence and, hence, the relationship between the parts. This is supplemented by projecting horizontal planes, forming small balconies together with red, yellow and blue painted 'sticks' forming supports and window transoms. The elevations are beautifully composed, again, like a Mondrian painting, to create a harmony within dissonance. The shift from the object to the relationship between the objects prefigures the later architectural language of Giuseppe Terragni, who was to harness the abstract in architecture a decade or so later.

Conceived as a concrete structure, the need for economy meant that the house was built of brick and covered in a cement render, which was then painted. When completed, at the cost some 17,500 guilders (the equivalent of around £100,000 today), it looked like nothing seen before and caused a stir. The Schröder children had to endure much teasing as the locals referred to it as the 'crazy house'.

With Truus's encouragement (and some financial support), Rietveld from that point on saw himself as an architect, not just a furniture-maker, and he went on to design over one hundred buildings. While he was not to repeat the significance of the Schröder House, he did continue with the use of abstract means in his designs to find his own voice. In 1955 he built a temporary open-air sculpture pavilion at the Kröller-Müller museum in Otterlo, near Arnhem, that was subsequently taken down. It was comprised of just five walls formed in concrete blocks and two horizontal planes (roofs). More abstract than even Mies van der Rohe's most minimal plans, it created a profound spatial experience. Thankfully, it was rebuilt ten years later and stands today as proof of Rietveld's creative genius beyond the Schröder House. His House Van den Doel in Ilpendam, built on polder land in 1958, stands as another of his masterpieces and a clear descendant of the Schröder House. Composed in volumes rather than planes and lines, it employs the colours of the natural materials – white, black, blue and green-grey glazed bricks, combined with concrete blocks – that leave an echo of De Stijl.

Rietveld used the garage space of Schröder House as his studio and worked closely with Truus from 1924 until 1932, when he moved to larger premises as his workload grew. He went home to his wife every night until her death in 1958, when he finally moved in with Truus to spend what proved to be the last six years of his life. In 1939, a ring road was built which passed close to the main facade of the house. In 1964, while Rietveld was living in the house, the road was converted into an elevated motorway. Cut off from the surrounding countryside, Rietveld had wanted to demolish the house but died from a heart attack on 25 June 1964,

SCHRÖDER HOUSE, UTRECHT, NETHERLANDS

the day after his 76th birthday. Truus Schröder stayed in the house for another 21 years until her death at the great age of 95 in 1985.

The house became a listed monument in 1976 and was consummately refurbished in 1986–7 by one of Rietveld's former assistants, Bertus Mulder. It was declared a UNESCO World Heritage Site in 2000. It is now a museum, run by the Central Museum of Utrecht, and attracts over 15,000 visitors each year. After more than 60 years living in the house, Truus Schröder was to describe her life there as 'the luxury of frugality'.

Gerrit Rietveld's
House Van den Doel,
Ilpendam, 1958

VILLA SAVOYE, POISSY, FRANCE

Le Corbusier, 1929

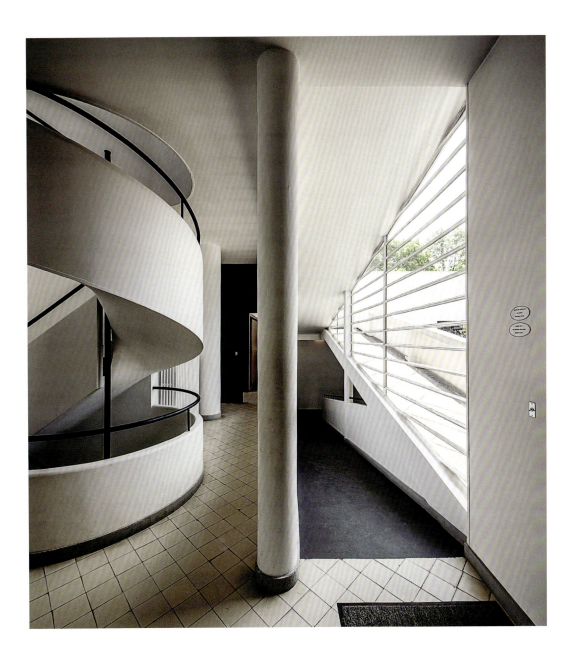

LE CORBUSIER'S CONVICTION AS a young man that he was destined to be not just a great architect, but the greatest, was remarkable. Born Charles Édouard Jeanneret-Gris in 1887, he worked in the studio of Auguste Perret in Paris, then Peter Behrens in Berlin, where he became fluent in German and was to meet Mies van der Rohe and Walter Gropius, all by the age of 23. He returned to his hometown of La Chaux-du-Fonds in Switzerland during the four years of the First World War, teaching at his old school while developing his vision for a new architecture to rebuild Europe after the first mechanised war in history. In 1920 he followed the art-world fashion of adopting a single name, 'Le Corbusier', based on his grandfather's name, Lecorbusier. Now he was ready to become not just a name, but a celebrity.

As early as 1914 at the precocious age of 27, Corbusier pursued the theme of mass-produced housing – from the outset he planned to change the world. He first proposed the Dom-ino system in 1914 – a name derived from *domus* (Latin for house) and the game of dominoes, revealing a talent for coming up with snappy names that would catch the imagination. This was little more than a concrete frame comprising six columns supporting three floors and was intended as a panacea after the destruction of the First World War, unaware as he was that it would rage for four years. With the Dom-ino frame, Corbusier developed his Five Points that codified the nature of the new world: buildings

VILLA SAVOYE, POISSY, FRANCE

were based on a structural frame free from constraints of limited spans, with *Les pilotis* (the columns) raising the house up into the air and away from the damp ground, *Le plan libre* (the free plan), *La façade libre* (the free facade), *La fenêtre en longeur* (the ribbon window) and *Le toit-jardin* (the roof terrace).

In 1918, he met the painter Amédée Ozenfant, a kindred spirit, and they published their manifesto *Après le cubisme*, boldly rejecting Cubism and establishing

OPPOSITE:
Exterior view of Villa Savoye

RIGHT:
Le Corbusier, 1942

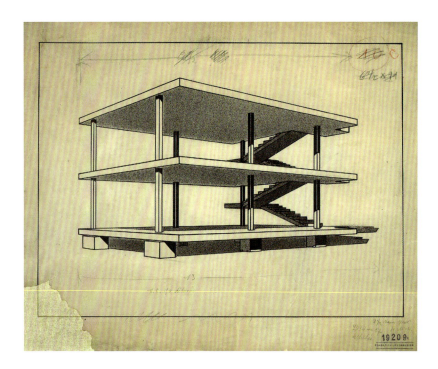

a new artistic movement: Purism. Together, they went on to establish the journal *L'Esprit nouveau*, many of Corbusier's essays for which were later to be incorporated in his book *Vers une architecture* (*Towards an Architecture*, mistranslated in the UK version as *Towards a New Architecture*) of 1923. This was to be the most influential book on architecture since Palladio's *Quattro libri dell'architecttura* (*The Four Books of Architecture*), published in 1570.

Corbusier developed his new architectural language over a number of years while designing a dozen houses, culminating in what is undoubtedly the seminal house of the 20th century: the Villa Savoye of 1929. As a pure work of architecture, it is a paradigm for an ideal, modern life, floating abstractly above its site, offering a new and healthy way of living. As a house, it failed to convince, for it was cold in winter, too hot in summer and, when it rained, it leaked badly and the pristine rendered walls slowly cracked and stained.

The 1920s was an era still in the shadow of the First World War, yet also a period of increasing industrialisation and urbanisation. Wealthy families such as the Savoyes could live and work in the city, but also escape to the country at weekends thanks to suburban railway links and the car. Living out of the city was part of the cult of health that had begun in Scandinavia and, ironically, in Germany with the Lebensreform movement from the late 1890s that promoted the virtues of fitness, the great outdoors and the sun. It became politicised by

VILLA SAVOYE, POISSY, FRANCE

socialists who thought it could lead to a breaking down of society and class. This gave rise not only to naturism, but also to sun clinics that opened in the belief that pure air and bright sunlight cured diseases such as tuberculosis. By the mid-1920s ('The Jazz Age'), sunbathing had become a cult for the elite.

Pierre and Emilie Savoye, perhaps lured by Corbusier's burgeoning reputation and wanting a prestigious and up-to-the-minute weekend house, approached Corbusier about building a country home in Poissy, then a rural outpost north-west of Paris, in the spring of 1928. Corbusier was a naturist and sun worshipper who believed that buildings should sit above the wet and damp of the earth, so in that sense he was a good choice for Emilie's brief for their country retreat. Pierre worked in an insurance company owned by his extended family, an odd client perhaps for what was destined to be the most progressive house in the world.

Corbusier's first scheme from September 1928 was founded on a square plan, one of the 'ideal forms', and was a full three storeys high with a central ramp slicing through the house. However, this was found to cost twice what the Savoyes were prepared to pay. It was redesigned to a smaller footprint, which abandoned the ramp, before Corbusier reverted to the original idea in the spring of 1929, persuading the Savoyes that the house could be built within their budget with a few minor modifications, including moving the master bedroom to the main floor from the roof where it had previously been placed. Of course, this was not to be, and the final cost was nearly 50 per cent over budget.

The final design was therefore founded on a square plan, although in reality it was a squarish rectangle. This was lifted up on *pilotis*, with ground floor

OPPOSITE:
Le Corbusier's
Dom-ino frame

BELOW:
Plan of
Villa Savoye

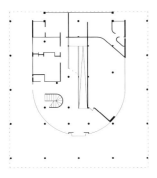

Ground floor

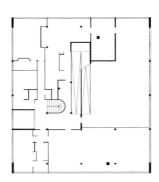

First floor

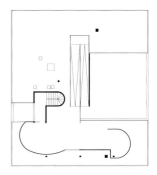

Second floor

accommodation for cars and servants recessed back from the supporting columns to allow a car to sweep under and around the house. This undercroft was painted a dark green, reinforcing the sense of the pure form floating above. One end is semi-circular and the dark green gives way to glazing set in vertical mullions, following the turning circle of the car, and the entrance is placed central to the curve. Entering into the house, the visitor is greeted by a long ramp directly ahead that scythes up through the floor above to daylight, while to one side a spiral staircase also invites ascent. A freestanding washbasin sitting on a sea of honey-coloured tiles suggests a ritual cleansing before ascending to the higher plane, as well as celebrating an industrial ready-made art object.

Ascending the ramp, the section of the house is slowly revealed as it slices through an outside courtyard before turning back on itself to arrive in a central hallway. The ramp provides not just an architectural promenade, but takes the journey from two-dimensional floor planes, through the floors on the third dimension and, in doing so, explores the fourth dimension – time. Exiting into the courtyard through a glazed wall, the ramp continues its journey up onto the roof.

The courtyard occupies nearly one-third of the plan and is enclosed by the external walls that are split by continuous, open, ribbon windows, framing

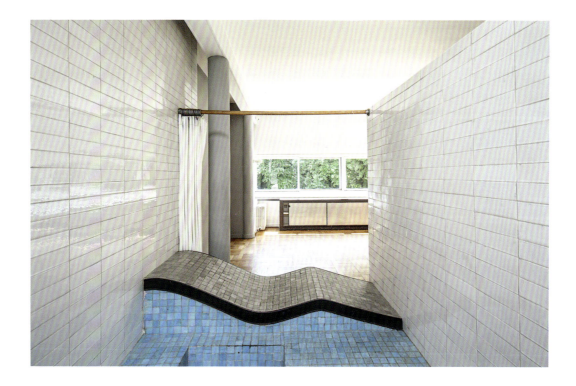

ABOVE:
Exterior view of the elevation of Villa Savoye

OPPOSITE:
The bathroom of Villa Savoye.

nature beyond, and the fully glazed walls of the ramp to one side and the main living space to the other. Here the walls of the building capture nature, both as an outdoor space and as framed views, all within man-made white abstracted planes.

Within, the house has all the usual Corbusian traits that he had worked out across the previous decade: a grid of columns floating across the space, strip windows, curved walls indicating ablutions, honey-coloured tiled floors, simple plastered wall finishes with planes picked out in muted primary colours, and the spiral staircase. Perhaps one of the key ciphers for the house is a built-in, sensuously shaped chaise-longue in Emilie's bedroom, hinting at the cult of health that she and her architect shared. With a black-tiled top above a bright blue-tiled base that incorporates a bath set into the floor, it forms something of a room divider between bed and bathroom, with a plastic shower curtain offering privacy. The promise of summer and health continues with the ramp, as it arrives on the roof to be embraced by curved screens creating a solarium – Arcadia at the top of the ascent.

Floating on its green site, surrounded by trees (although its sylvan isolation was to be severely compromised after the site was bought in 1958 by the neighbouring school), the villa is a beguiling, Platonic, Purist edifice. A 'pure' white box lifted up on slender columns, with a sybaritic rooftop, like the Parthenon

33

atop the Acropolis, or perhaps an ocean liner. It became known as *Les Heures Claires* (Blue Skies) and the promise of a new health-inducing lifestyle in touch with nature was compelling.

ABOVE:
Villa Savoye before renovation in *c.*1950

OPPOSITE:
Yvonne Gallis with Le Corbusier in *c.*1930

The reality was to prove less agreeable. By June 1930 Emilie Savoye wrote to Corbusier saying that, 'It is still raining in our garage' – this followed previous correspondence pointing out several leaks in bedrooms and bathrooms. This launched a fiery exchange with the contractor who had warned Corbusier about the architect's details and refused to accept responsibility. The situation persisted as the house suffered further leaks, exacerbated by condensation and humidity, probably made worse by a faulty heating system, and so the relationship between client and architect, with both unwilling to accept any blame for the problems, soured. 'It is raining in the hall, it's raining on the ramp and the wall of the garage is absolutely soaked . . . it's still raining in my bathroom, which floods in bad weather, as the water comes in through the skylight. The gardener's walls are also wet through' wrote Emilie. After two further years, with the Savoyes' son Roger admitted to a sanatorium for his poor health that they blamed partly on the conditions at the villa, and in frustration, Emilie wrote again, 'After innumerable demands you have finally accepted that this house which you built in 1929 in uninhabitable . . . Please render it habitable immediately. I sincerely hope that I will not have to take recourse to legal action.'

The situation was never resolved during the less than ten years before the Savoyes fled Paris at the outbreak of the Second World War. During the German occupation, the villa was used by the occupying army as a hay store and, upon liberation, by the Americans, who shot out all the windows upon leaving. The Savoyes returned after the war but were unable to fund the restoration so they abandoned the house. The derelict villa was taken over by the town of Poissy in 1958 and some repairs were carried out, using it as a youth centre before making plans for its demolition to make way for a school building. Worldwide protests from architects, and Corbusier himself, saw the building saved by André Malraux, the French minister for Cultural Affairs.

The same year that the villa was completed, and after a ten-year courtship, Corbusier finally married the Monaco-born fashion model Yvonne Gallis. They agreed not to have children as that would interfere with his devotion to his

VILLA SAVOYE, POISSY, FRANCE

art, although it would have been unlikely anyway as she was already in her late thirties. Despite this, he continued to have several affairs, most famously on a ten-day journey aboard a cruise ship from Buenos Aires, where he fell under the spell of the Afro-American entertainer and actress Josephine Baker (one of his sketches of her nude recently sold for $12,000). Yet Corbusier seemed devoted to Yvonne and he was clearly dependent on her in his own way.

The Villa Savoye has been one of the most influential buildings of modern architecture, in fact, in history. It spawned endless copies by lesser architects across the world, although technology for flat roofs quickly improved, but in cooler climates it would take until the 1970s to understand the problems of condensation that gave rise to wet ceilings, even though roofs were in fact watertight. For Corbusier, however, it was the end of the line for his 'white villas', and he was never to employ slender *pilotis*, ribbon windows and white walls again. His restless search in many ways paralleled that of Picasso, who dominated the art world in the 20th century; following his groundbreaking *Les Demoiselles d'Avignon* in 1907, Picasso developed Cubism with Georges Braque before moving on to other forms of expression after 1914. So too Corbusier moved on after the Villa Savoye to buildings founded more on primitive and regional associations. The Pavillon Suisse and Cité de Refuge projects quickly followed, using concrete and rubble fused with industrially produced metal frames. Perhaps the Purist dream, when translated into the Villa Savoye and left out in the rain to peel and crack, made Corbusier turn back to the elemental.

VILLA MÜLLER, PRAGUE, CZECH REPUBLIC

Adolf Loos, 1930

IN 1908 ADOLF LOOS PUBLISHED his essay entitled 'Ornament und Verbrechen' ('Ornament and Crime') in Vienna. It delivered an attack on the current German Werkbund that was trying to integrate art into industry and the Secession (Art Nouveau) style that dominated architecture and the applied arts across Europe. He was to write that 'The German Werkbund has set out to discover the style of our age. This is unnecessary labour. We already have the style of our age . . . the evolution of culture marches with the elimination of ornament from useful objects.'

In this prescient polemic, Loos laid a foundation for a new ideology that was inherited from the Arts and Crafts movement and would prove to be fundamental to the development of the Bauhaus and modernism. His philosophy held that ornamentation caused objects to go out of style and so become obsolete, and for him this was immoral, or 'degenerate' in his language. He held that buildings should be honest, free of the superfluous and not beholden to style – a polemic he carried across many walks of life, from cooking to menswear. Despite a congenital loss of hearing which meant that, by his fifties he was using a hearing trumpet, he held court at the cafe tables in Vienna where he counted other great Viennese minds such as Arnold Schoenberg, Ludwig Wittgenstein and Oskar Kokoschka as friends. He was clearly an engaging man and was renowned for his good sense of humour. He established a reputation more as an intellectual, philosopher, writer and teacher than an architect until he was able to demonstrate his ideas with his Steiner House of 1910, which was to cause a stir with its austere, stripped-down classical form. This was not due to a process of abstraction but rather of functional expression, devoid of decoration.

With a commission to build a store for the Viennese tailors Goldman and Salatsch in the Michaelerplatz, in the heart of old Vienna opposite the Imperial Palace of the Hofburg, Loos became something of a celebrity. The overt simplicity of the design caused a great

RIGHT:
Adolf Loos in c.1939

controversy that ended with a municipal order to suspend work, but this was overcome with the support of the highly regarded architect Otto Wagner, despite Loos's previous criticism of his work. Finally completed in 1911, the building was stripped of all decoration and became known as 'the house without eyebrows'. Allegedly, Emperor Franz Joseph I of Austria left his palace by another gate to avoid seeing this naked aberrance.

Loos insisted on the necessity of freeing civilisation from the superfluous and the avoidance of waste. He was interested in necessity – every object in day-to-day life should be subjected to the rigid laws of suitability to purpose, of *Sachlichkeit* imposed by utility. In later years, his young wife Claire wrote of his

VORTRAG
VERANSTALTET VOM AKAD.
ARCHITEKTEN VEREIN.
ADOLF LOOS:
ORNAMENT
UND
VERBRECHEN.
FREITAG, DEN 21. FEBRUAR 1913,
½8h ABENDS IM FESTSAAL DES
ÖSTERR. ING. U. ARCH. VEREINES,
I. ESCHENBACHGASSE 9.
KARTEN ZU 5, 4, 3, 2, 1 K
BEI KEHLENDORFER
12. MÄRZ:
MISS LEVETUS: ALTENGL. KATHEDRALEN.
MITTE MÄRZ:
DR. HABERFELD: ÜBER ADOLF LOOS.
DRUCK A. BERGER WIEN VIII/2

VILLA MÜLLER, PRAGUE, CZECH REPUBLIC

outrage at wasting soap (anticipating the plot line of Gabriel Garcia Marquez's 1985 tragic-comic novel *Love in the Time of Cholera*): 'Don't you know', he cried at her, 'that I have spent my entire life fighting against the senseless, against ornamentation, against the waste of energy, against the waste of material'.

Adolf Franz Karl Maria Loos was born in 1870 in Brünn in the Moravian region of the Austro-Hungarian Empire, now Brno in the Czech Republic. He failed to complete his studies and went to the United States aged 23, living with relatives in Philadelphia for three years. He did many different kinds of work, from dishwashing to bricklaying and, having mastered the English language, journalism. Having toured around the great eastern cities of America, his visit to Chicago, where he witnessed the Columbian Exposition, made an enduring impression on him that the new world of modernity was imminent. He saw the machine, or industrialisation, as a true emblem of the *zeitgeist*.

Returning to Europe, he settled in Vienna in 1896 at the age of 26 to devote himself to architecture. He worked for a building firm and, within a year, he started to publish numerous and challenging essays in the '*Neue Freie Presse*' of Vienna that were to result in 'Ornament and Crime'. In 1920 he held the post of Chief Architect for the housing department of Vienna but resigned after two years when he moved to France, dividing his time between Paris and the Riviera while making frequent trips back home to Vienna and Brünn. With his reputation among French avant-garde circles bolstered by the republication of 'Ornament and Crime' in the pages of Corbusier's and Amédée Ozenfant's *L'Esprit nouveau*, he became an honorary member of the Salon d'Automne.

He married an actress, Lina Obertimfler, in 1902, but divorced three years later. He was later to marry the 20-year-old dancer Elsie Altmann in 1919, a union that lasted a full seven years before he fell in love with another dancer, Bessie Bruce. Finally, he married the 24-year-old photographer Claire Beck when he was 59, in poor health and chronically deaf. Divorced just three years later, he died the following year aged 63. Poor Claire was to write a fond memoir of her time with Loos three years after his death but, at the outbreak of war, she was interned with her mother at Theresienstadt in 1941, then deported to Riga and killed on arrival on 19 January 1942, at just 37 years of age.

Loos was decidedly a ladies' man, but he seemed to remain on good terms with all his wives while flirting constantly with other women. He never had a bank account, begged money from his clients, even years after a commission was completed, and preferred to keep his money in his jacket pockets as he lived in fear of the tax authorities. He lived the high life but was ultimately to

OPPOSITE:
Poster advertising a lecture by Adolf Loos on 'Ornament and Crime', 21 February 1913

die destitute. Aldo Rossi was to write that he saw Loos as a template for Robert Musil's *The Man Without Qualities*, one of the most significant novels of the 20th century, yet there was also a darker side to Loos. He stood trial twice for child pornography and molestation, first in 1908 and later in 1928 when he received a suspended sentence.

From the Steiner House in 1910 across the next 20 years, Loos was to build a handful of houses. In 1922 he built the Rufer House in Vienna and this was to be the first design that evidenced his principle of *Raumplan* – a spatial planning approach, sizing volumes according to their need and importance so the house became a kind of giant Jenga puzzle of interlocking volumes. The *Raumplan* was to reach its culmination in Villa Müller, which was destined to be his last major residential commission. Loos was to write that,

> My architecture is not conceived in plans, but in spaces (cubes). I do not design floor plans, facades, sections. I design spaces. For me, there is no ground floor, first floor etc . . . For me, there are only contiguous, continual spaces, rooms, anterooms, terraces etc. Storeys merge and spaces relate to each other. Every space requires a different height: the dining room is surely higher than the pantry, thus the ceilings are set at different levels. To join these spaces in such a way that the rise and fall are not only unobservable but also practical, in this I see what is for others the great secret, although it is for me a great matter of course. Coming back to your question, it is just this spatial interaction and spatial austerity that thus far I have best been able to realise in Dr Müller's house.

Built in the northern hills in the suburbs of Prague on a sloping site which commands panoramic views, the house was commissioned by Dr František Müller and his wife Milada Müllerová. Dr Müller was an engineer who co-owned a construction company called Kapsa and Müller which was an early pioneer in reinforced concrete construction techniques. Dr Müller was, like Loos, a leading light in the Czech society of the day so they were a natural fit.

The site has an 11 m (36 ft) north-facing slope with the house sitting high up in the south-west corner. It is commanding and stark – a white cubic form with small scattered windows, with only the north face looking towards the old city given a solemn symmetry, where three tall windows indicate the main living level, and a square central aperture above which has a reciprocal projecting balcony.

Plan of Villa Müller.

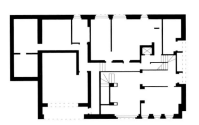

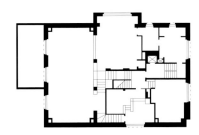

Ground floor

Raised ground floor

The house is reached by a public staircase along its western side that was partly funded by Dr Müller. This leads to a recessed entrance, lined in yellow travertine, that folds to create an inviting bench set between an oak front door and a stone cube that has a bowl of geraniums covering an aperture for sending coal down into the cellar. Opening the door, the contrast with the austere exterior is startling, as the walls are clad in vibrant emerald green glass panels that zing off the orange earthen floor tiles and a bright orange-painted radiator. Off the lobby and decorated with purple walls and vibrant yellow furniture lies a small reception room to deal with visitors who were to be kept away from the private realm.

Loos's opposing views on 'ornament' within the private realm of a building seem perplexing, yet he held that 'The building should be dumb on the outside and reveal its wealth only on the inside'. For him the outside belongs to 'civilisation', whereas the inside belongs to the 'individual'. His work sought to protect the private sphere from public morality.

From the lobby, a stair winds up a half level to enter into the main living space through a framed and stepped wall clad in a greenish-grey lightly veined Cipollino de Saillon marble. It is an enormous room of classical proportions that straddles the entire front of the house, some 11 x 5.6 m (36 x 18 ft) in plan and 4.4 m (14 ft 5 in) high. The room has three tall windows with bright yellow silk curtains, but no doors, allowing it to link to the spaces and varying floors beyond the marble-clad wall. The room has an intensely English country house feel, everything where it should be – brick fireplace, brass pendant lights, mahogany furniture, oriental rugs and, curiously, no communal seating, only solitary chairs.

From the living salon, up another half flight of steps and to one side lies a dining room, a lower, darker space with a highly lacquered mahogany coffered

Villa Müller, main hall

ceiling and a beautifully crafted circular table sitting on an octagonal base that seats six diners but can be enlarged to sit up to 18. Continuing Loos's pleasure in English design there are 18th-century Chippendale chairs that he saw as paradigms of utility – but only one original as the others were copied with enormous skill by craftsmen in Prague. The interiors not only vary in volume but also in light, with some areas being quite dark for a modern house.

Moving through the house is like walking through a three-dimensional maze, with each room on a different floor and each of varying proportions and decor. The oak staircase assumes an imaginary axis of the house, while other staircases lead to other parts and it all culminates in a large roof terrace, with a framed view across to St Vitus Cathedral at Prague Castle.

When completed, the Müller House was the culmination of Loos's *Raumplan*, setting out new territory from the Corbusian free plan with its interlocking of volumes within the shell of the building. It would be another 21 years before the dominance of the free plan would be challenged again, when Louis Kahn's Trenton Bath House in the US ushered in the return of 'rooms' as discrete spaces. The house was also one of the first to bring natural materials to the internal realm as a decorative finish in itself, along with Mies van der Rohe with his Tugendhat House that same year.

The Müllers lived happily at the house and, as they were half German, the house was not confiscated during the war, but was later seized by the Communists in 1948. Dr Müller was to die in the house when he unknowingly inhaled carbon monoxide while stoking the boiler. His wife stayed on, living in a few rooms from 1959 until her death in 1968 when the house was taken over by the state as a cultural monument as well as being used for storage, as a library and then later by the Institute of Marxism-Leninism. After the Velvet Revolution the house was returned to their daughter Eva Maternová but, as she was no longer living in Czechoslovakia, she sold it to the Municipal Office of the City of Prague and the villa became the property of the City Museum in 1995. The house was declared a National Cultural Monument that same year and was restored in 1998 and finally reopened as a museum in 2000.

The *Raumplan* died with Loos, although his legacy was to be seen as a prophet for modernism, as his early insight into the utility in design – free of the superfluous and not beholden to style – was to be taken up by the succeeding generations.

TUGENDHAT HOUSE, BRNO, CZECH REPUBLIC

Mies van der Rohe, 1930

SUCH IS THE FATE OF SOME of the great houses of the 20th century that they only serve as a home for a brief part of their existence, and this was the case with the Tugendhat House, which was occupied by the family that built it for less than eight years. Completed in December 1930 in the city of Brno in Czechoslovakia – the birthplace of Adolf Loos – it was commissioned by Fritz and Grete Tugendhat who were German Jews. Grete was a divorcee with a young daughter and heir to a textile, sugar and concrete empire, who had met and married Fritz Tugendhat. Fritz was, by all accounts, a hypochondriac and a mild-mannered man, so Grete held sway in their relationship and pushed him into running part of the textile business, while he dreamt of being a photographer. While living in Berlin during her previous marriage, Grete had visited the Villa Perls, an early work of Mies van der Rohe from 1911, designed in the style of Karl Friedrich Schinkel, while he was employed by Peter Behrens. She later had also visited the Weissenhof Exhibition of 21 buildings in Stuttgart built for the Deutscher Werkbund in 1927, and had been impressed with Mies's apartment block, so when her wealthy parents gifted her part of the site of their Art Nouveau villa as a wedding present, she sought out Mies to design the new house.

Mies, as he became commonly known, was born Maria Ludwig Michael Mies. He added the 'van der' from the Dutch as the German 'von' was restricted to those of aristocratic lineage, and his mother's surname, 'Rohe'. He had begun his career working in his father's stone carving shop in Aachen, perhaps engendering his love of craft. He carried out his apprenticeship in architecture in Behrens's office from 1908 to 1912, where he was to meet Walter Gropius and Corbusier and experience the progressive design theories of Behrens. His talent meant that he quickly gained independent commissions for large upper-class homes and, from the beginning, he rejected the purely classical styles that were then common and sought a way to design houses that

TOP:
Mies van der Rohe in c.1930

BOTTOM:
Grete and Fritz Tugendhat in c.1930s

The front exterior of Tugendhat House.

were relevant to the time. He admired the neoclassical work of Schinkel, with its use of simple cubic forms and repetitive elements.

Mies was physically a big man, taciturn and reticent in character, rarely seen without a fat cigar; he drank prodigiously and treated his women carelessly, leaving his wife and two children for his mistress, only to then leave her behind in Berlin when he fled to America as war loomed. From 1926 he became vice president of the Deutscher Werkbund – a group dedicated to integrating art and industry in design that prefigured the Bauhaus, which he also went on to head in the 1930s. In 1933, when the Nazis closed the Bauhaus, Mies lobbied party officials for three months until they agreed to reopen the school, but on the condition that two of its left-wing teachers, Ludwig Hilberseimer and Wassily Kandinsky be replaced with 'individuals who guarantee to support the principles of the National Socialist ideology'. Mies gathered his staff and closed the school.

There followed a period when Mies tried to gain work from the state, even signing a motion of support for Hitler in the August 1934 referendum, and was shortlisted to build the state's new Reichsbank, but this was lost when Hitler discovered the young Albert Speer and catapulted him to chief architect for Joseph Goebbels's propaganda ministry before enlisting him as his Hitler's personal architect, to give form to his megalomaniac vision of a new Reich to last for a thousand years.

Mies travelled to Brno in September 1928 and was impressed by the Tugendhats' site, which occupied the end of a long park opposite the Spilberk, crowned by Brno castle. By Christmas, Mies called to say the design was ready and, on New Year's Eve, Grete and Fritz visited him in his studio in Berlin and stayed until the early hours, missing the evening's celebrations. Grete recalled years later how much they liked the design, although her husband was initially shocked and doubted the large open living space. Persuaded by his wife, they did, however, ask for three concessions: that the steel columns on the upper floor be hidden into the walls; that a bathroom be made en suite to the master bedroom; and that all windows be provided with sun screens as they feared overheating in the summer months – all of which Mies agreed to.

The building was to be in brick, but Mies resorted to white-painted render after finding that a there was a lack of skilled labour and no decent bricks available. Construction started in the spring of 1929 with the Brno firm of Artur and Moritz Eisler, and the steel frame came from Germany.

Arriving on Černopolni Street, the house appears as a sleek, low, flat-roofed building – certainly different from its context, but not unfamiliar to those who followed the architectural trends of the day – set back from the street behind a steel fence. It has three elements: an almost blank solid wall (save a single high-level strip window to one side) to the east terminated by a muscular chimney stack; this is then mirrored, as if its negative, with a light, open form set beneath a wide-spanning roof edge; and a third, box-like element that projects forward, terminated by a large garage door to the street which completes the composition.

The use of three rectangular forms, arranged together to form a composition, had been used by Mies on a few of his previous projects, such as the Wolf House, completed in 1927, and here provided two rectangular blocks containing bedrooms, linked by a glass entrance and a detached garage block that contained accommodation for a chauffeur. The ensemble is held together by a broad terrace and the roof plane hovering above, with a single column hinting at the entrance, tucked in behind the opaque glazed wall that ends in a semicircular prow. While the arching roof offers a framed view through to the world beyond, the milky glazed wall hides what lies within and the front door is blank, creating a sense of anticipation. Once within, a large, empty entrance hall awaits, with only the travertine flooring and a wall of dark timber lending a sense of domesticity and promise of more to come. Within the curved end of the glazed wall is a staircase, pivoting around a chrome-clad column, descending to the level below.

Descending the staircase and turning, the house is suddenly revealed as a vast, shimmering space, given order by a regular grid of shiny columns that exist between a slightly ochre-coloured linoleum floor and a smooth white ceiling. In Simon Mawer's 2009 Man Booker Prize shortlisted novel, *The Glass Room*, the Tugendhat House takes on a fictional identity as the 'Landauer House' and the main space is beautifully described: 'And all around them is the Glass Room,

The entrance hall of Tugendhat House

a place of balance and reason, an ageless place held in a rectilinear frame that handles light like a substance and volume like a tangible material and denies the very existence of time'.

The main living space is vast, at 237 sq m (2550 sq ft). Mies had been developing his ideas for 'free space' since his somewhat prophetic Country House plan from 1923, inspired by Cubism, the art of De Stijl and the experiments of the Russian constructivists, where space is not enclosed by walls but rather defined by the spaces between walls – walls that never meet. In the 'Glass Room'

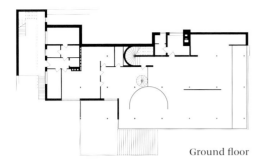
Ground floor

First floor

of Tugendhat House, with full-height glazing on two sides, space is divided up by free-standing partitions, given autonomy by their materiality. A thin partition, some 6 m (19 ft 6 in) long and 7 cm (3 in) thick, formed in onyx slabs from the Atlas Mountains, carefully spaced away from the columns, incises the plan laterally, dividing the main living area to the front from a study space to the rear. To the other end of the room a semicircular partition clad in Makassar ebony partially encloses a dining space, replete with circular table.

To the eastern end of the house, where the full-height glass wall wraps around the corner, the fenestration changes to create a half grid, which is taken up by a conservatory, bringing nature within the building. The glass wall itself was engineered with great skill to drop into the floor so that it formed a balustrade to the room by means of a hydraulic system within the basement, allowing the room to be completely open to the southern side, so further dissolving the line between inside and outside – between man-made and natural.

Not since the work of Adolf Loos in the first decade of the century had modernist architects employed the nature of materials – the quality of stone, metal, wood and fabrics – to enrich space in the way that appeared at the Tugendhat House. This was not the Corbusian dream of mass-produced, white architecture but the continuation of a craft tradition, the love of materials and the precision in their use, both technically and spatially. Working with his partner Lilly Reich, much as Charlotte Perriand did with Corbusier's furniture designs, a more domestic, feminine touch was introduced, with Shantung silk curtains, colourful oriental rugs and bespoke furniture. The contribution of Reich has been airbrushed out of many histories of architecture, which tended to concentrate on the 'big man', yet from 1925 when they began their relationship, both personal and professional, until Mies left for the United States in 1938, their work was highly collaborative and, while he undoubtedly was

ABOVE:
Plan of Tugendhat House

BELOW:
Lilly Reich in the 1930s

The interior living space of Tugendhat House

behind the singular, precision design concept for the buildings, she was the key influence on the materiality that was to lend the work such richness.

This precision can be seen in the design of the columns, where Mies utilised four standard steel angles, placed back to back to create a cruciform, which is then clad in German engineered, precision-moulded chromium plates with rounded edges. They not only define an orthogonal grid through their cruciform shape but also, with no base or capital, reinforce the sense of a continuous, homogenous space, almost as if it is an aquarium with light shimmering between the luminous columns. Mies, with his devotion to philosophy, much as Louis Kahn was to espouse a few decades later, has become codified by a few aphorisms, such as 'Less is more' and 'God is in the detail'. Years later, with his New National Gallery in Berlin of 1968, he managed to make a single coda – the cruciform – dictate not just the detail of the columns, but the chairs, as well as the overall building itself, while at the Tugendhat House the complexity of the columns manages both to define a structural order while at the same time offering the simplicity of dissolved, universal space.

At the same time as the house was under construction, Mies was to design and complete the German Pavilion for the International Exposition in Barcelona – now known as the Barcelona Pavilion. Completed in 1929, the Pavilion was to establish Mies's burgeoning reputation as one of the leaders of the Modern Movement. It used the same principles as the Tugendhat House but, free of the need to be occupied, the architectural vocabulary was stripped back to two horizontal planes set 3 m (9 ft 9 in) apart – floor and roof – supported by the same cruciform, chrome-clad columns and three free-standing walls in opulent materials; onyx, travertine and green Tinian marble.

'I have striven for a series of spatial effects', Mies wrote, and these spatial effects made the 'Glass Room' at Tugendhat House the most complete and startling domestic space in its day. In 1930, this was the most avant-garde house in the world. With the final cost at some 5 million Czech crowns, enough to build many hundreds of workers' houses, Prague's artistic activist Karel Teige called it 'modernist snobbery', denouncing the Tugendhats for building, in 'the spirit of fancy baroque palaces, the seat of a new financial aristocracy'. This had some truth as the house contained the ultimate luxury of a 'Mottenkammer', a moth-resistant storage room for fur coats.

With the rise of the Nazis and their lethal anti-Semitism, dark clouds gathered across Europe, so Mies, as well as the Tugendhats, made plans to leave the country. Mies left Berlin and his partner Lilly Reich for good in August 1938 for Chicago, where he became head of the architecture department at the Armour Institute (now the Illinois Institute of Technology, or IIT). His wife Ada, from whom he had separated in the early 1920s, stayed behind in Berlin with their teenage daughters. In March 1938 Hanna, Grete Tugendhat's daughter by her first marriage, was sent to England to join her father and shortly afterwards Grete left Brno with her two sons for Lugano

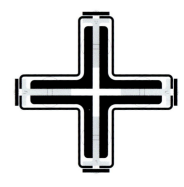

ABOVE:
Horizontal column section of Mies van der Rohe's German Pavilion, Barcelona, 1929

BELOW:
View from the garden towards Tugendhat House

Rehabilitation Centre,
February 1959

in Switzerland. Fritz joined them later that year and, three years later, they escaped further to Venezuela.

In October 1939 Tugendhat House was taken over by the Gestapo, who knew a good thing when they saw it, and in the autumn of 1940 a German soldier and ex-architecture student, Louis Schoberth, stayed in the house. He became friends with Gustav Lössl, the Tugendhat's chauffeur who remained in the house up until the beginning of September 1941. By January 1942, it became a prized possession of Nazi Germany and the aircraft designer responsible for the feared ME109 fighter, Willy Messerschmitt, moved into the house as it became the offices of his aeroplane works which had moved to Brno out of reach of Allied air raids.

As the Nazi terror overstretched itself and the powers of the Allies, the Americans and the Russians prevailed, the Red Army of Marshal Rodion Malinovsky liberated Brno in April 1945, when Russian bombardments shattered the glass walls of the Tugendhat House. It became the home of a Russian cavalry unit that stabled its horses in the 'Glass Room', where the horses did considerable damage to the linoleum floor and the windows. After liberation, it became home to the private dancing school of Karla Hladká, an instructor at the Brno Conservatory that lasted until June 1950. The house was placed under the ownership of the Czechoslovakian state in October 1950 and became a rehabilitation centre for children with spinal defects as part of the nearby children's hospital up to the end of the 1960s.

The house underwent renovation between 1981 and 1985 but was to be fully restored under the expert guidance of the youngest daughter of Fritz and Grete, Daniela Hammer-Tugendhat along with her husband, Professor Ivo Hammer, during 2003–5. The house today is a UNESCO World Heritage Site hosting thousands of visitors each year.

DALSACE HOUSE (MAISON DE VERRE), PARIS, FRANCE

Pierre Chareau, 1932

AS THE GERMANS ROLLED into Paris in June 1940, the Jewish architect and furniture designer Pierre Chareau fled, initially to Portugal, then Spain and Morocco, before arriving in New York later that year. Ten years later, having failed to revive the career that had made him celebrated in France, he committed suicide on 24 August 1950.

Chareau had made his name with the Dalsace House, immortalised as the 'Maison de Verre' ('House of Glass') completed in Paris in 1932. It was the first building to capture the dream of the translucent house which culminated in Mies van der Rohe's Farnsworth House some 19 years later. In some ways, it echoed a new conception of space that was introduced to the world in 1851 by the Crystal Palace at the Great Exhibition in London with its vast cathedral-like, ethereal volume of delicate iron and glass that undoubtedly changed everything.

Pierre Paul Constant Chareau was born in 1883 in Bordeaux and, for a man who was to build one of the greatest houses of the 20th century, he remains

OPPOSITE:
Interior view of
Dalsace House

ABOVE:
Pierre Chareau by
Therese Bonney in
the 1930s

something of an enigma – unlike many of the greats, he wrote little, published less and was it seems a diminutive, quiet and modest man. What is known is largely down to accounts left by his friends and his wife Dollie (born Louise Dyte in England). They met when he was just 16 and she 19, marrying five years later.

It is thought that Chareau graduated from the École des Beaux-Arts in Paris in 1908, probably not as a regular student, but perhaps following evening courses. He worked for the large British firm of Waring and Gillow from 1899, a firm that specialised in furniture and interior design, until he was subscripted into military service in 1914. After nearly five years of enduring the horrors of the First World War that saw some 600,000 French casualties alone, Chareau survived to begin his independent professional career in 1919 after discharge from the army at the age of 35.

Essentially, Chareau became a furniture designer with an empathy for the British designs that he had seen in Hermann Muthesius's *Das Englische Haus* published in 1904, as well as the more innovative designs of C.F.A. Voysey and Charles Rennie Mackintosh. By 1920 Chareau had developed his own distinctive style in his furniture designs, with a leaning towards mobility – pieces that partly or wholly moved – and a fascination with transparent and translucent materials such as glass and perforated metal, together with an anthropomorphism that perhaps came from aspects of form combined with mobility. His art deco design for an 'office library' in the French Embassy for the Pavillon de la Société des Artistes Décorateurs was shown at the Exposition Internationale des Arts Décoratifs et Industriels Modernes in Paris in 1925 and received great praise, in particular for his use of sliding screens that allowed the modulation of lighting levels.

In 1928, in collaboration with the Dutch architect Bernard Bijvoet, he took on a commission for a clubhouse in Beauvallon, near St Tropez. Built in reinforced concrete, it reveals little of what was to come in Paris, although it was started the same year, leading to the false assumption that Bijvoet was the lead designer (particularly as it bears striking similarities to his 1931 Zonnestraal

ABOVE:
Exterior view of Dalsace House

OPPOSITE:
The main salon of Dalsace House

Sanatorium in Hilversum, designed with Jan Duiker), while Chareau took on the interior and furniture design.

In 1927 Dr Jean Dalsace, a gynaecologist, and his wife Annie were gifted a property upon their marriage; a town house in the rue de Saint Guillaume, hidden from the street within a courtyard. Annie imagined a new modern house, but an elderly woman on the top floor refused to move out and, protected as she was by Parisian tenancy laws, the decision was taken to insert a new house into the existing carapace, leaving the top two floors in place. Chareau's wife Dollie was Annie Dalsace's English and dance teacher so, when she was looking for an architect, she did not have to look far.

Arriving at No 31, rue de Saint Guillaume, there is no hint of one of the century's greatest houses, just a typical 18th-century, four-storey Parisian terrace with a large pair of timber doors to the street. These open into a small courtyard, only about 10 x 10 m (33 x 33 ft), where the house suddenly appears. It is startling – with no walls, no windows – rather a screen of glass blocks. Ever since

the Crystal Palace, architecture had become familiar with glass walls. Walter Gropius had pioneered the curtain wall with his Fagus Factory in 1910 and Bruno Taut had built his Glass Pavilion in 1914 at the Cologne Deutscher Werkbund Exhibition. What appeared at the Dalsace House was not a glass house as such, but a translucent screen, perhaps more reminiscent of a traditional Japanese house. It is not a pavilion structure with four sides and a roof: only the front and back facades are of glass.

Set within a beautifully proportioned frame of slender, black-painted steel, containing panels of 20 x 20 cm (8 x 8 in) glass blocks, four wide and six high to work with a 91 cm (3 ft) module that runs through the entire design, Chareau created a facade of 40 bays. The square glass blocks each have a circular lens so that the rectilinear nature of the ensemble has a secondary counterpoint. The ground level has a black canopy above a recessed entrance, with storey-height clear glass panels indicating entrance and life within. Another five and a half bays of framed glass blocks return to one side and also indicate domestic life, with two strips of clear glazed windows to the upper floors. The glass block facade creates a sense of mystery, a wonder at what lies behind – it is a veil that tantalises and, at night, it becomes a giant lantern.

Once within, the house continues to baffle, as layer upon layer of translucent and transparent screens appear. Riveted steel columns that hold up the upper floors provide one of the few reference points to stability as every wall and screen seems to slide and turn, open and close. A grey, studded rubber floor leads to a reception for Dr Dalsace's ground-floor surgery – fronted by metal-framed glass screens that pivot open to expose the rear glass facade and a strip of windows that reveal a garden beyond. The plan is intense with no clear diagram, rather a lattice of intricately planned spaces that open and close into themselves. The reception and waiting room are placed centrally, with the servants' quarters to the one side. To the other side lie the doctor's consulting rooms and a double-height office at the rear onto the garden. The reception and waiting room are placed centrally, with the servants' quarters to the far side. A spindly, tubular steel-framed staircase that finds support only top and bottom outside the doctor's consulting rooms leads directly to his private study above.

Another staircase is buried within the servants' quarters, while the main stair by the entrance is enclosed by glass and perforated metal screens, with two doors, one curved and the other straight, that separated family life from patients. This staircase is simply beautiful with its broad, studded, rubber-covered treads that, without risers, perch almost invisibly on twin girders recessed beneath. To each side, ankle-height tubular balustrade rails hint at security, with no other handrails on offer. Chareau liked to refer to this beautiful invitation to ascension as his 'monumental ladder'. It climbs towards the light of the main glass block facade as if floating, making ascent an ethereal experience.

Leaving behind the somewhat disorienting hall of mirrors with diaphanous screens slipping and sliding, the main stair climbs gently to arrive in the main salon where suddenly the house makes sense, for it reveals a magnificent double-height space with seven riveted-steel supports holding up the apartment above and fronted by the glass-block screen filtering light into the room. Grey-studded rubber flooring and built-in furniture provide the backdrop here, with a metal-framed bookcase occupying the entire wall opposite the staircase, which itself is surrounded by bookshelves that double-up as balustrading. The upper gallery is open, but with three-quarter height storage cupboards held on a steel lattice. To the short return of the glass-block wall, a tall array of mechanical, white-painted metal panels that are connected by arms and driven by a wheel, like a submarine chamber, provide ventilation. Generally, metal elements are painted black, save some vertical reinforcing bars to the facade and the riveted-steel columns that are painted in a vibrant vermillion orange, with the outer flanges clad in black slate.

The salon is inhabited by several items of Chareau's furniture that ironically look dated – upholstered, somewhat art deco sofas and chairs, a small wooden table, a folding screen, a large easel and a grand piano that was used by Annie Dalsace to entertain guests. To the rear of the space another sliding screen

Detail of the bottom of the stairs of Dalsace House

closed off the doctor's private study and rest area. Off to one side, set behind the staircase lies a dining space, backed by a curved wall. Shelving, screens, pivoting shelves, revolving cupboards, curtains and rosewood furniture abound.

Chareau was, like Gerrit Rietveld, first and foremost a furniture designer. While Rietveld took the spatial ideas of De Stijl and extended them into habitable space, Chareau extended his love of detail and play of materials into creating a house. A desk he had designed for his own apartment in 1927 ('Desk MB673') clearly demonstrates his design approach, fusing metalwork (he had begun working with the metalwork craftsman Louis Dalbet in 1924) and timber. Its restless angular form – folding and cantilevering as if it were in motion – is set within a thin metal framework formed in flat sections, utilising its inherent strength to attain a delicate balance, supporting horizontal timber panels and a small cupboard suspended to one side. The same approach can be found time and again at the Dalsace House, perhaps most clearly evident in the bookshelves that form a balustrade around the gallery of the main salon (and appear again, with cabinets, on the second floor).

Another staircase, this time with a tiled finish, lies parallel to the main flight and climbs up to the second floor. It has a landing, lined with further versions of the bookshelves, that wraps the void, allowing glimpsed views down into the salon. The rear of this floor lies behind a wall of shiny black lacquered, subtly curved full-height panels – some opening into storage cupboards, others into the bedrooms. This rippling black wall is seductive and hints at sensuous goings-on beyond within the three bedrooms. In fact, in turns out that the bedrooms are almost occluded by Chareau's devotion to ablutions – the rooms are splayed in plan and within each, set upon a low plinth, are curved enclosures made from perforated metal, with curved sliding screens, partially concealing basin and bidet (that also partially rotates to accommodate the user). The black-painted perforated screens are spaced off the plinth and are door height, so appear as cubicles within the room. The beds themselves sit on a 1.8 m (6 ft) wide, slightly taller plinth running along the rear glass block wall – but this time, with mid-height clear glazed windows – the majority of the room is left to act as a day room, with chairs and a writing desk.

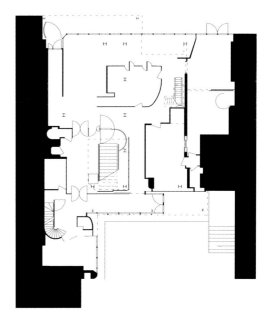

Plan of Dalsace House

It is the master bedroom suite to one side that provides one of the most eccentric, intense, yet beautiful rooms in the house. One enters the room straight into a master bathroom that is the same size as the two other bedrooms but split by a three-quarter-height central screen, again formed in curved panels of brushed aluminium concealing shallow storage spaces for towel racks and the like. To one side lies a rectangular enclosure for basin and bidet, while to the other is an extraordinary free-standing aluminium cupboard with four curved faces that all open like an exotic flower to reveal drawers in perforated metal. This gives proof to Adolf Loos's declaration in 1924, 'Imagine this: a closet is nothing more than a kind of case for precious ornament'. A second basin and a bath fill the space, while a bulging wall reveals a circular shower enclosure. As if as an afterthought, through a sliding door lies the bedroom itself, which turns out to be almost a normal rectangular room – plastered surfaces and carpeted floors, with a built-in curved rosewood drawer unit brought from the Dalsaces' former apartment – and a double bed in the centre of the space. A smaller daybed

DALSACE HOUSE (MAISON DE VERRE), PARIS, FRANCE

sits at right angles against the rear, glazed wall set upon a low, black-tiled plinth. Alongside this is a small retractable staircase that seems to offer escape to the day room below.

The house is a tour de force of detail with almost every piece lovingly designed and made – even visible screws were handmade on site. It can therefore be exhausting to walk through as there is nowhere that does not call for attention (and then admiration), but take a seat in the salon and it is the diaphanous light, like being underwater, from the glass-block facade that leaves a lasting impression.

While the house was being built, Annie Dalsace reported seeing Corbusier, by then celebrated for his Villa Savoye, several times peeking in across the courtyard. He must have enjoyed witnessing this *machine d'habiter*, yet here his analogy became fact, as Chareau's house became almost literally a machine, with his fascination for moving parts. Within a year of the completion of the Dalsace House, Corbusier built his apartment block in rue Nungesser with its glass-block facade (with inset ribbon windows).

The Dalsace family finally moved into the house after four years' work and a cost of some 4 million francs (the equivalent of £5.5 million today). It became a salon, regularly playing host to French Marxist intellectuals such as Walter Benjamin (Jean Dalsace was a member of the French Communist Party) and the artists Jean Cocteau, Yves Tanguy and Joan Miró.

After the Dalsace House Chareau became celebrated, yet with France in the grip of a recession he struggled to gain work and did not build another house before he left the country in 1940. He did, however, amass a large collection of contemporary art, from Picasso to Modigliani, without realising the eventual value these would one day command.

The house was rediscovered in the 1960s by a young group of British architects – notably Richard Rogers and Norman Foster – and their fascination with its transparency and its internal mechanisms lead to the rise of the 'high-tech' architecture that abounds across the world today.

The Dalsace House was eventually occupied by the Chareaus' daughter Aline and her family, until it was sold to the American businessman and collector Robert Rubin in 2006, who has lovingly restored the house and generously allows tours from time to time.

FALLINGWATER, BEAR RUN, PHILADELPHIA, USA

Frank Lloyd Wright, 1937

WHEN FALLINGWATER HIT THE PRESS in 1938, its architect, Frank Lloyd Wright, was to grace the cover of *Time* magazine, where it announced Wright as 'the greatest architect of the 20th century'. Wright was a master publicist, his own greatest fan, and never shy in coming forward to remind the world of his genius, yet he too was surprised at the praise and worldwide acclaim for this house.

The house is magnificently photogenic, perched daringly above a waterfall with horizontal terraces that defy gravity and the water seemingly gushing through the house itself. This was perfectly captured by the 25-year-old photographer Bill Hedrich, who went into the nearest town and bought a pair of waders so that he could stand in the middle of the icy-cold Bear Run river to capture the drama of the house – a view that had already been anticipated in a perspective drawing by Jack Howe in Wright's studio two years previously. This photograph caught the world's imagination, ending Wright's professional drought of nearly ten years during the Great Depression.

Wright is perhaps best described as the last great Victorian architect. Born in 1867 in a small farming town in Wisconsin as Frank Lincoln Wright, he changed his middle name to Lloyd after his parents' divorce when he was 14, in honour of his mother's family who had emigrated from Wales – the Lloyd Joneses.

BELOW:
Jack Howe's colour drawing of Fallingwater

OPPOSITE, TOP:
Frank Lloyd Wright, 1954

OPPOSITE, BOTTOM:
Edgar Kaufman in his downtown office in c.1940

FALLINGWATER, BEAR RUN, PHILADELPHIA, USA

At the age of 21, he became an apprentice in the office of Adler and Sullivan, where he stayed for five years. Louis Sullivan was to be one of the fathers of the Modern Movement and part of a group that became known as the 'Chicago School'. Following the great fire of 1871 when Chicago was almost completely destroyed, new technologies appeared that allowed multi-storey construction: the steel frame, telephones and the first passenger lift. Architects like Sullivan embraced these innovations and created a new architectural language that was based on the expression of the frame itself. Wright was to depart from the firm when Sullivan discovered he had been moonlighting on a series of house projects, which was forbidden by his contract. So, at the age of 26, Wright began his own practice, mainly building houses that spawned the 'Prairie Style', a series of extended low houses with shallow pitched roofs and terraces that thrust out into the landscape.

Some 50 houses and 15 years later, Wright was commissioned to rebuild the Unity Temple that had burnt down in 1905 in the suburb of Oak Park in Chicago. Completed in 1908, this proved to be one of the most significant buildings in the United States in its day, and one of the first reinforced concrete structures in 20th-century architecture. Its cubic forms were to inspire European architects, in particular the Dutch De Stijl group, as one of its founders, Robert van't Hoff, had worked briefly with Wright in 1913 and went on to build the first reinforced-concrete house in Europe, the Villa Henny near Utrecht, in 1916.

By the time Wright met Edgar Kaufmann, his client for Fallingwater, he was 67 years old and his career had slumped, having built only a couple of houses since the completion of the Imperial Hotel in Tokyo in 1923. His reputation as the trailblazer for a modern American architecture had faded and the avant-garde had shifted decisively to Europe and the work of Corbusier and the Bauhaus architects, leading to the International Style. Wright, convinced of his supremacy, made his distaste for 'the Internationalists', as he called the European Moderns, into a personal crusade which merely made him seem to be the last of the old guard, hanging on to the past. In fact, Wright's architecture was incredibly progressive and inventive, founded on a belief in nature rather than the abstract concerns of the Europeans.

Kaufmann was born into a successful merchandising family founded on department stores fuelled by the industrial might of Pittsburgh at the turn of the century. At the age of 24 with his marriage to his cousin Lillian (who later changed this to the more sophisticated 'Liliane'), the daughter of his late uncle, Isaac, he consolidated control of the Kaufmann dynasty. In an era when the department store became a major force in popular culture across the United States, Kaufmann was a natural in spotting emerging fashions in merchandising and display. He was able to set trends and the Kaufmann store became a kind of social hub, offering a glitzy promise of the future with escalators, elevators and large seductive shop windows. It was perhaps his talent for publicity and spotting trends that led him to Wright, although it has been contested that it was Kaufmann's son Edgar Jnr who brought the two great men together. Edgar Jnr had spent time at Wright's architectural school at Taliesin in 1934, but only for five months rather than the usual two to four years, with rumours that Wright would not tolerate his alleged homosexual activities.

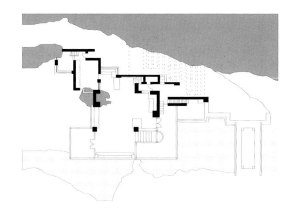

ABOVE:
Plan of Fallingwater

OPPOSITE:
Section of Fallingwater

Wright first visited the site of Fallingwater in December 1934, staying with Kaufmann at his house in Pittsburgh, just ten days before Albert Einstein was also a guest there before delivering his first scientific lecture in the United States. They entered into an unlikely friendship: the Jewish Kaufmann beguiled by Wright's talent, yet having little understanding of 'modern' architecture; and Wright anti-Semitic and pompous with a disorganised way of working – particularly when it came to his perennial lack of funds and frequent demands for money. Kaufmann had to wait until late September 1935 – a full nine months' gestation – until Wright famously produced all the drawings in two hours flat, watched by his apprentices in the time it took Kaufmann to travel to Taliesin. This outpouring of genius is a beguiling story, yet records show that Wright had over many months worked out the form of the house and had indeed prepared his client for the startling location of the house set over the waterfall.

It is tempting to think of Fallingwater as Wright's riposte to the International Style that had been canonised in the 1932 Museum of Modern Art exhibition

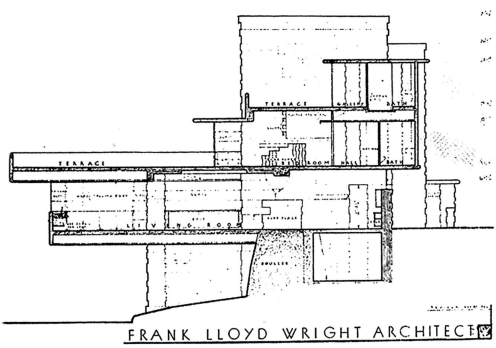
22. Section of house, looking west.

in New York, but Wright denied this: rather, he saw it as a continuation and an evolution of his earlier work that he called 'the constantly accumulating residue of formula'. The plan was indeed a development of his Prairie houses, with the basic organisation of a cruciform penetrating a square, along with a spiralling perimeter and hidden entrance. The embryo of the design can be traced more directly back to his Gale House of 1909 that utilised the flat roofs of the Unity Temple and, crucially, reads as a series of horizontal trays – balconies and a roof – that project across the front, while an earth-bound chimney anchors the house to the site. This composition of balancing horizontal elements against the vertical is the essence of Fallingwater, where dramatic cantilevered balconies and projecting roof edges are visually held into a balanced composition by a vertical stone chimney structure.

In the plans produced on that morning, the underlying order of five parallel walls and piers standing on the rock ledge was established. Above, the order is less evident as the walls fragment and disappear, taking form as a series of thick

ABOVE:
Fallingwater from the south-west

OPPOSITE:
The living space of Fallingwater

masonry walls that stagger across the back of the house in a series of zig-zags that never quite touch, an abstract layout bringing to mind a De Stijl painting or Mies van der Rohe's Country House plan from 1923.

To place the house above the waterfall, Wright anchored it to a narrow ledge between the hillside and the stream with a concrete structure of three columns (rather than four on his original sketch plan), each with a diagonal 'bolster' that supported the main floor and projecting balcony above. This then extended to some 18 x 24 m (59 x 79 ft), far exceeding the available site below. Wright stacked a further two floors above and it seems surprising still to realise that the house is one of his tallest at four storeys, or 12 m (39 ft) high. He was to separate the Kaufmanns across the floors, with Liliane's bedroom taking pride of place on the second floor, Kaufmann's bedroom off to one side and their son Edgar Jnr's bedroom on the third floor – all united by a chimney stack. This arrangement reflected not only Kaufmann's Victorian attitude towards marriage, but also what was undoubtedly a dysfunctional family, as personal relationships between the Kaufmanns were not all they seemed from the outside, with Kaufmann routinely taking new lovers while plying his wife with gifts. It seems ironic, therefore, that the whole structure should revolve around a symbol of family unity, the fireplace, when they were all in fact so isolated from one another. Wright gendered the composition in a Victorian manner with Liliane's balcony providing the house with horizontal strength, while the rooms of the male

FALLINGWATER, BEAR RUN, PHILADELPHIA, USA

Kaufmanns lend vertical strength in the stone tower that carries their bedrooms.

Wright was to write in his biography, regarding his 1923 Imperial Hotel in Tokyo and its structural approach of cantilevering floors, 'Why not then carry floors as a waiter carries his tray on upraised arm and fingers at the centre – balancing the load?' His structural intuition proved to be right as the hotel survived a catastrophic earthquake in 1923, only to be demolished 44 years later to make way for a high-rise structure.

There is an also undeniable European influence at work in this composition, perhaps garnered from two of his former employees who had both come to the United States from Austria; Rudolph Schindler in 1914 and Richard Neutra, who arrived in 1923. Both had variously worked in Wright's office between 1920 and 1925 and both had gone on to build a couple of celebrated houses in California. Schindler's Lovell Beach House at Newport of 1926 may be seen as a clear precursor to Fallingwater, with its series of horizontal balconies supported on vertical columns with splayed supports picking up the cantilevers, but this was also a very European affair with its white rendered, International Style overcoat. Neutra's later Lovell Health House in Los Angeles of 1929 was the most European-style house in the United States at that time and attracted enormous notoriety. Again, it employed long horizontal balconies that floated across its site as the main form of expression.

There is no shortage of books on Fallingwater that provide a highly detailed account of every space, catalogue every feature and artwork, and give a

blow-by-blow account of the difficult construction, the ballooning costs and the often-tortured relationship between Wright and Kaufmann. Yet it is hard to find any account that dares to question the great man's creation.

Walking into the main space after slipping in quietly through the back door (which is in fact the front door), its general proportions are unexpected for the room is very deep, dark and low, although the ceiling does have a raised section in the middle. The strip windows across the front and sides, with double doors out to the two flanking balconies, provide a glare of light against the riven stone slabs of the floor and striated stonework to the walls, but there is no view of the stream, only a ribbon of trees can be seen. The waterfall can be heard, but the water of Bear Run can only be seen towards the front of the space through a glazed hatch that offers a suspended staircase down to the stream. Walking out onto the terraces, the sound of water increases but it can only be seen when peering over the alarmingly low balcony walls. Of course, placing the house above the stream and waterfall means that the occupants cannot see the water from the living spaces, and this is somewhat frustrating. It shows that Wright was most concerned with the drama of his design rather than the experience of living in it.

Wright furnished the living room with various built-in seating areas but again they all turn their backs to the view. As with all of Wright's houses, the fireplace is a triumph; an enormous cave-like construction in coursed stone with a vast iron grate and even a large spherical drum that could be swung over the fire to heat mulled wine. In front of this, the boulders that Kaufmann once used to sunbathe on now form a hearth, more than 2 m (7 ft) long and heaving out of the floor into the room, fulfilling Wright's philosophy that 'it is in the nature of any organic building to grow from its site, come out of the ground into the light . . .'

The stone walls, with varied course depths and with thinner courses often projecting to provide ledges for books or ornaments, form the back of the house, offering a reassuring cave-like refuge from the nature visible to the front of the house, but they feel somewhat heavy and insistent. Externally, the stone tower, partially bisected by thin horizontal slabs towards the top, lends visual weight to make the whole house feel stable and the chimney is split away from the stone corner by a three-storey high window that evokes a Japanese folding screen. With horizontal members every 42 cm (17 in), this window sets up a strong counter-rhythm to the vertical stone stack and is lent a further touch of

FALLINGWATER, BEAR RUN, PHILADELPHIA, USA

Exterior view of Fallingwater taken from the living room

elegance by the fact that the glass has no frames at the wall junctions, but is simply built into the stonework, and by the ladder of casements that open to leave an invisible corner.

If the interior of Fallingwater is less successful than its beguiling exterior, there remains another slightly discordant aspect in the final finish of the external horizontal balconies and roof edges, for these are a curious colour – an ochre that has too much flesh tone to be earthy. Maybe it is intended to reflect the feminine horizontal, but actually it has a strange sense of something fruity and organic, not concrete or earth. Of course, they could never have been white as not only would this not concur with Wright's organic philosophy, but it would have been far too European. Interestingly Wright had originally proposed these be covered in gold leaf, like the quiet gold of Japanese screens, but Kaufmann was nervous that his customers back in Pittsburgh would think this too extravagant, so a waterproof cement paint was chosen. It remains tempting to imagine how extraordinary the house would have looked encased in golden carapace, shimmering above the water.

VILLA BIANCA, SEVESO, ITALY

Giuseppe Terragni, 1937

GIUSEPPE TERRAGNI WAS TO DIE in somewhat mysterious circumstances on 19 July 1943, on the steps of his fiancée's house in Como, northern Italy, at just 39 years of age. Six days later, a *coup d'état* deposed the Fascist leader Mussolini and led to Italy's withdrawal from the Second World War. Terragni had served with the Italian army on the Russian front as a captain in the artillery and, after commanding barrages 'against little more than teenagers', he suffered a breakdown. Following a spell in a military hospital, he was returned to Italy in January 1943 to convalesce. A friend described him during his last days as 'no longer the old Terragni: he seemed invaded by mystical manias; he would leave his house simply to go to a friend to ask forgiveness for having said who knows what who knows when. And one of those days he went instead to his fiancee, and on the stairs, his heart gave out.' Today, we understand the severity of what is now called post-traumatic stress disorder and perhaps, as many believe, Terragni took his own life, unable to come to terms with the horror of his actions serving the Fascist regime.

Terragni had been born on 18 April 1904 into a family of builders, but his strong artistic talent led him to study at Milan Polytechnic, where he graduated in architecture in 1926. He grew up and worked in the lakeside town of Como and started a practice there with his engineer brother Attilio in 1927. Their first large commission was the Novocomum apartment block in Como that was completed in 1929. This building was to establish Terragni as something of a leader of the avant-garde architects in northern Italy and was included in the Weissenhof Exhibition in Stuttgart, and later exhibited in Rome representing the Movimento Italiano per l'Architettura Moderna: it is now considered to be the first work of Italian rationalism.

BELOW:
Giuseppe Terragni in the 1930s

Terragni's early work was clearly influenced by the white villas of Corbusier but overlaid with a concern for classical geometry: in particular, his designs were underpinned by the Golden Ratio, known by Renaissance artists as the Divine Proportion. This proportion throws up one of the most magical ciphers in geometry and resonates throughout nature – a proportion of 1.618, where in the case of a rectangle it can be subdivided into a perfect square and a smaller rectangle that has the same ratio as the rectangle it was cut away from.

RIGHT:
Giuseppe Terragni's
Casa del Fascio,
Como, 1936

This harmonious geometric relationship ties Terragni back to Italian classical tradition and, while this is an aesthetic principle rather than a mathematical or empirical truth, it lends meaning and depth to his work.

By 1928 Terragni had joined the National Fascist Party and served in the army. His brother became mayor of Como and his party-political connections undoubtedly led to their commission for the Casa del Fascio (House of the Fascists) that was to be completed in 1936. This was to be Terragni's masterpiece. After the Second World War, with the benefit of hindsight, it seems hard to imagine that Mussolini's brief for this modest palazzo was to be a 'glass house', open and democratic, with nothing between the leader and his people. Sited just outside Como's city walls and facing the apse of the cathedral, it symbolised a new order against the ancient church and state. It was the first building Terragni designed which sat on an open site. Its form was a double cube of a perfectly square plan with a central atrium placed asymmetrically, and at ground level the central space ran through the whole building from front to back, closely corresponding with the classical Venetian palace plan. The double cube was formed by a framed structure that gave order to all the facades and, while each was different, the frame gave unity. While a very modern framed structure, Terragni held to his classical roots in cladding the frames and walls in marble.

The front facade is the most simple and monumental, offering a five-bay, four-tiered colonnade to the city, juxtaposed with a blank wall. At the foot of the colonnade was a series of 16 synchronised glass doors that would all open out in unison, allowing the Fascist Guards assembled in the atrium inside to march out onto the plaza, while a single entrance door sat at the end of this array behind the blank wall. This facade reveals a wonderful ambiguity in Terragni's architecture, at once classical yet modern, it also reads simultaneously as a solid

LEFT:
Exterior view of Giuseppe Terragni's Casa Giuliani Frigerio, Como, 1939

OPPOSITE:
JPA plan of Villa Bianca

cubic form that has been hollowed out – a subtractive process – and as a layered composition – an additive process. This compositional richness is such that the elements – walls, windows, doors and so on – become so absorbed into the overall composition that they become abstracted; an architecture that creates relationships between the various parts that form it. Peter Eisenman, one of the New York Five architects, demonstrated this perfectly in his study of Terragni's 1939 Casa Giuliani Frigerio apartment block in Como, published in *Casabella* in 1970. This illustrated how the building had a series of geometric forms, and how various parts of the design shift to occupy these forms, creating almost tangible relationships between the parts – like the paintings of De Stijl where it is the relationships between the geometric blocks of primary colours that create space and movement in the work, rather than the actual blocks themselves.

The Villa Bianca was completed a year after the Casa del Fascio and was built in the Terragni ancestral hometown of Seveso, set between Milan and Como. Commissioned by his cousin Angelo, an engineer and building contractor, and named after his daughter who had died young, it was to be the first of a proposed residential development that was never realised. This was to be an even deeper exercise in the square, the Golden Ratio, shifted planes and volumes, and local symmetries. It is, however, the raised-up entrance portico that is pulled out, like a drawer, from the main volume, and the enormous frame that wraps it and captures the entrance ramp beyond, that make this uniquely a work of Terragni.

VILLA BIANCA, SEVESO, ITALY

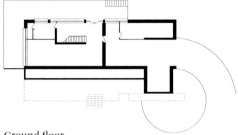

Ground floor

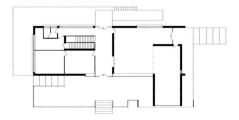

First floor

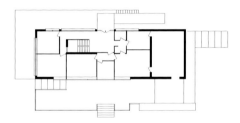

Second floor

Villa Bianca is clearly heavily influenced by Corbusier, with its white-rendered facades and ribbon windows within a long rectangular form – three cubes joined together – that runs parallel to the street in a north–south orientation. It sits on its site without *pilotis*, although the ground floor is raised by a half level over a part basement containing garage, laundry, boiler room and servant's quarters. A small set of steps lead onto a terrace where the entrance is set exactly halfway along the east facade. This opens into a large hallway which divides the plan in two. Another exit leads to a stepped ramp that drops back down to the garden. From this nascent *piano nobile*, a large living space takes up the north end of the plan, with a studio jutting out to face the street, while to the southern end lies a dining room that connects directly to a kitchen and pantry.

At first floor, bedrooms are set behind a series of ribbon windows, but to the north end a large terrace within the volume of the house is carved out and contains a second stepped ramp that snakes up to a vast rooftop terrace. The upper terrace is given expression by the use of two parallel raised concrete awning structures, or cornices, that cantilever out beyond the front and rear walls to the south and north respectively. To the street, the incised lower terrace juts forward above a projecting box containing a studio below, clad in a grey stucco, presenting a window onto the street. This element appears as if pulled out from a larger aperture that reveals the terrace above and is in turn surrounded by a concrete frame, or sleeve, that is clad in a grey Beola stone to its outer faces. Period photographs capture the rich layering of this device as slender poplar trees are captured between the frame and the main house. This idea of push and pull, of surrounding elements in concrete sleeves, is quintessentially Terragni and was to reach its climax in his small Asilo Infantile Sant'Elia school in Como, completed the same year.

While the concrete sleeve and cantilevered awnings supported on a grid of columns suggest the house has a concrete frame, in fact it does not, rather it is built using solid concrete walls, with cut-out apertures. The walls are painted in a very light grey (rather than Corbusian white), and windows are given a classical touch with marble-lined reveals.

As a house, the plan of Villa Bianca is not remarkable, it is the abstraction with classical overtones and the striking roof awnings that make the building truly innovative. Terragni created a sophisticated essay in geometry from what at first appears to be a standard International Style rectangular box. With the captured and projecting studio on the front elevation, it appears as if frozen a millisecond after it has exploded, with hidden volumes bursting their way out of the box. It is the space between elements that make his work so intelligent and abstract.

On 11 November 1938, on the eve of war, Terragni and the Como architect Pietro Lingeri were summoned to the Palazzo Venezia in Rome for an audience with Mussolini to discuss a commission for a museum dedicated to the 'Greatest of Italian poets', Dante Alighieri. The Danteum, as it became known, was planned for the proposed exposition of 1942 but, in the summer of 1939, with Mussolini signing the Pact of Steel with the Nazis, it was shelved until 'more favourable days'. The design was Terragni's richest and most poetic work and, if built, despite its associations with fascism, would surely have joined the pantheon of the world's greatest monuments. Generated from a Golden Ratio rectangle (the long side being equal to the short side of the Basilica of Maxentius) and two overlapping squares, the design held a geometric and mathematical correspondence to Dante's *Divine Comedy*, which had a structure of three canticles of 33 cantos each, plus an introduction, making 100 cantos. The building became an 'architecture of literature', a journey through a series of spaces, from an entrance court of 100 columns (Dante entered a forest in Canto 1 of the Inferno), to Purgatory, ascending up to a Paradise, a room of

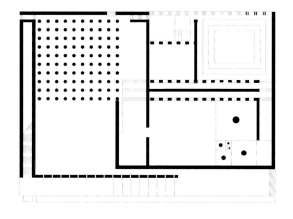

TOP:
Exterior view of Villa Bianca

BOTTOM:
Plan of Giuseppe Terragni's unbuilt Danteum, Rome

VILLA BIANCA, SEVESO, ITALY

33 glass columns holding up a glass roof and, finally, to a room dedicated to the new Roman empire. It anticipated in its dense narrative and symbolism the later works of Corbusier and Louis Kahn. However distasteful the associations with fascism, this was Terragni's most complete demonstration of the relationship between the abstract and the figurative.

Terragni had a short life and he only completed 14 buildings, many working alongside his artist friend Mario Radice in Milan and Lingeri, but that is still a remarkable achievement in a profession where success favours those with more years. Radice was to say of Terragni that 'His was not a normal existence, but more or less a life with a mission, with his thoughts fixed in the direction of art . . . He was totally wrapped up in Architecture, having no time for anything else; parties, sport, vacations, were excluded from his life; it was as if he had a secret premonition of an early death.'

In 1949, six years after his death, a commemorative exhibition was held in Como and was opened by Corbusier, who stopped in front of the Danteum project and said, 'This is the work of an architect'. Terragni's later reputation was blighted by his connection to the horrors of fascism, but he was to influence a new generation after the war when Bruno Zevi published his work in the 1960s, and later Eisenman rediscovered his genius to inspire the New York Five. The Villa Bianca was used as restaurant for many years but has recently been renovated and is occupied again as a private house.

Postcard of Villa Bianca, c.1938

VILLA MAIREA, NOORMARKKU, FINLAND

Alvar Aalto, 1939

HUGO ALVAR HENRIK AALTO WAS BORN in 1898 in Finland, a country then under Russian rule. Although neutral during the First World War, the Jaeger Movement was formed that opposed Russian rule. In 1916 the young Aalto enrolled in the School of Architecture in Helsinki and soon found himself arrested and imprisoned for a few weeks as a suspected member of the Movement. He was, however, not interested in politics at that time, writing to his father that, 'I'm a hell of a liberal and an oppositionist in theory, in practice I'm an architect and generally top man'.

Following the February Revolution in Russia in 1917, the Finns declared independence and civil war broke out the following year between the 'Reds', who wanted their own Communist Finnish state, and the 'Whites', who sought compromise and negotiation with Russia. Both Aalto and his father soon found themselves second in command of a White regiment and both saw action before the eventual defeat of the Reds in May 1918.

Resuming his studies in a now independent new nation, Aalto was one of seven of the original 11 students in his year group at architecture school who survived the ordeal. His early work was firmly set within the Nordic classicist movement that was led by the Swedish architect Erik Gunnar Asplund. He set off to Stockholm in the summer of 1920 confident that he would find work with Asplund, only to find that there was no place for an inexperienced young Finn in his office. While there, he did strike up a lifelong friendship with Sven Markelius, who was a friend of Asplund's and had good social connections that were going to be important in years to come.

BELOW:
Alvar Aalto at his desk in 1945

Completing his studies the following year, he then served his military service and was finally released in the summer of 1923 when he returned to his hometown of Jyväsklä. He decided to set up his own practice at the precocious age of 25 in a single room in the basement of the finest hotel in town. As commissions slowly grew, he persuaded a young architect, Aino Marsio, from a local practice to jump ship and join him – and within the year they were married. Aalto liked to joke that he had no choice but to propose to Aino as he owed her

VILLA MAIREA, NOORMARKKU, FINLAND

TOP:
Alvar and Aino Aalto in the 1950s

BOTTOM:
Exterior view of Alvar Aalto's Paimio Sanatorium, 1933.

much in unpaid salary, but in truth they were kindred spirits and complementary – he outgoing, impulsive and often reckless, she calm, quiet and organised. She ran the practice as his equal.

Aalto was a country boy but had enormous confidence and charm, so made friends easily, and he slowly shook off his provincial manners and dress. He was highly competitive and was an excellent gymnast, priding himself on his physical fitness (he was to start every day with an exercise routine throughout his life). Lacking work, his self-belief drove him to enter architectural competitions, initially without much success and producing no income. But, in the spring of 1927, he entered two competitions and won them both – followed that year by five more that he did not win. That summer, buoyed by his undiminished self-belief, he decided to move to Turku, the former capital of Finland, on the coast, linked to Stockholm by ferry.

Despite the couple's perilous finances, they embarked on a European tour in the summer of 1928 to visit Jan Duiker's Zonnestraall Sanatorium – then under construction – and Hilversum Town Hall, Jacobus Oud's housing in Rotterdam, and Corbusier's Villa La Roche in Paris and Villa Stein at Garches. From this point on, Aalto left behind the Nordic classicist style and embraced functionalism.

Aalto continued to make competition entries, no less than 34 in the 10 years from 1923, and failed most, but in 1930 he finally turned the corner with a design for a new tuberculosis sanitorium in Paimio, not far from his new office in the south of Finland. This building was to launch his international career upon completion in 1933. It was a large building, to house nearly 300 patients, and on first sight it appears as an International Style, flat-roofed, white-rendered building. Aalto planned the building in separate departments within distinct wings of varying heights, all angled from each other in plan to respond to the views, the terrain and the sun, and this made it distinct. Dominated by a slender and very long, seven-storey wing that contained the wards and was topped by a roof terrace that allowed patients' beds to be wheeled out to the sun and fresh air, it was the epitome of Corbusier's healthy living ideal. Its rational architecture was carefully adjusted to the site in an almost organic way. In section, too, curves and splays found their way into the building, adding a human touch. Aalto had found his unique take on the purely functional.

The building was published around the world and the *Architect's Journal* in the United Kingdom announced, 'At 35, Aalto has taken modern architecture beyond the good and evil of that German fetish, functionalism. He has infused its bare bones with a vital human spark and reasserted the dignity of the human scale without the least concession to adventitious ornament.'

The sanitorium project was, however, unable to solve the couple's finances as the Great Depression swept across Finland, so they moved again to Helsinki at the end of 1933, leaving unpaid rent in Turku. Once again using his network of friends, Aalto was quickly able to enter the inner social circles of the city. Through his friend Nils-Gustav Hahl he was to meet Maire Gullichsen, the daughter of Walter Ahlström, one of Finland's leading industrialists. Maire had studied art in Paris between 1925 and 1928 and had met and married Harry Gullichsen upon her return.

Hahl and Maire Gullichsen set up an avant-garde gallery for modern art in Helsinki to act as a focus for progressive culture. By the time Aalto met Maire in 1935, she was 28 and had also established her own Free Art School as an alternative to the Academy. It was a meeting of minds and the Aaltos and Gullichsens became firm friends. Maire undoubtedly saw in Aalto a man who was ahead of the field and recognised his talent. Aalto quickly found himself in a commercial partnership with the country's leading patron of the arts, backed by the Ahlström wealth. They formed Artek, the company now famed for the manufacture and distribution of Aalto's glassware and furniture.

With Harry Gullichsen providing commissions, 1936 turned the corner for the Aaltos with a competition for the Finnish Pavilion at the Paris World Fair of 1937 – Aalto was so desperate to win that he submitted two entries, winning first and second place! The winning scheme, a series of timber-clad pavilions that stepped down a slope to envelop a courtyard full of trees, was an apt representation of Finnish forests. Aalto was to fall out with the sponsor, the Minister of Trade, who wanted a wide range of Finnish products exhibited, whereas Aalto stuck to young, progressive products summarised in large black-and-white photographs – and, of course, a wide range of Artek furniture and glassware – so he finally refused to attend the opening ceremony. But the Pavilion found praise from

VILLA MAIREA, NOORMARKKU, FINLAND

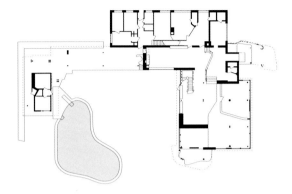

Plan of Villa Mairea

Corbusier himself, who commented that, 'In the Finnish Pavilion, the visitor is delighted by its deep-rooted authenticity. It has been a point of honour for the authorities to choose the right architect.' At this point in his career, Corbusier had left the white villas behind in favour of a search for culture and authenticity.

In the autumn of 1937 Harry and Maire Gullichsen were to ask Aalto to build them a summer house on part of the Ahlström family estate in Noormarkku, 200 miles north of Helsinki on the west coast of Finland. Their brief was to provide a house for entertaining and relaxing, incorporating space for Maire's burgeoning art collection and an office for Harry – but it was also to be an expression of modern life, asking Aalto to 'regard it as an experimental house; if it did not work out, we wouldn't blame him for it'. Given such a free hand, it seems surprising that Aalto struggled at first, initially producing a rustic design based on Finnish farmhouses resulting in Maire's exclamation that, 'Well, we asked you to make something Finnish but in the spirit of today'.

In early 1938, Aalto, like much of the world, was struck by Wright's Fallingwater and immediately tried to persuade the Gullichsens to build their home over a stream on a different site. Unable to persuade them, he developed several sketch designs that owed a clear debt to Fallingwater, with cantilevered decks and rock-like basement storeys. Finally settling on an L-shaped plan, the Gullichsens approved the design and, in the spring of 1938, work commenced on site.

With a plan that provided a series of rooms – gentlemen's room, ladies' room, library, music room, ping-pong room, winter garden, art gallery – it was far from progressive and Aalto, and perhaps Aino too, was discontent, so with foundations being laid and accepting the basic plan form, they set about redesigning the house. The plan of what became known as the Villa Mairea became centred on a large reception room containing various functions. With the art gallery removed, art was integrated with life.

A 7 m (23 ft) deep, curvaceous projecting canopy leads to the entrance, opening into a small lobby. An angled wall guides the visitor to turn left and rise three steps to enter into a large, open reception space some 14 x 14 m (46 x 46 ft). With an earthy quarry-tiled floor and a finely grooved timber ceiling, the eye is immediately drawn diagonally across to a large fireplace that occupies

the corner of the room. A pair of shiny, black-painted steel columns huddle together in the middle of the space and are wrapped in rattan halfway up. Looking left, the same space continues but the floor changes to timber and one corner is enclosed by a wall that stops short of the ceiling – although a series of undulating glass louvres bridge the gap – to enclose the library. Behind the fireplace lies a winter garden that Maire used for flower arranging and where a small staircase led up to her studio.

The main staircase occupies the final corner parallel to the entrance steps, in the crux of the L-shaped plan. This stair is a miracle; a cluster of circular red pine poles, irregularly grouped to enclose and support the staircase. The treads are wedge-shaped pine, each with carpet coverings secured by brass rods that in turn sit on three steel stringers. Each tread seems to float and, with fixing brackets clamped to the poles at different heights as the stair rises, the poles recall the growth rings of bamboo, so that the entire staircase begins to feel like a plantation – even the handrails curl around the base of the poles like tendrils.

Beyond the staircase, a long, narrow dining room runs back into the plan, forming a zone between each arm of the L shape, and this in turn provides a terrace above at first floor. The wing running back behind the dining room contains office, staff rooms and kitchen. The dining space continues back towards

ABOVE:
Exterior view of Villa Mairea

OPPOSITE:
Drawing of Villa Mairea by Alvar Aalto

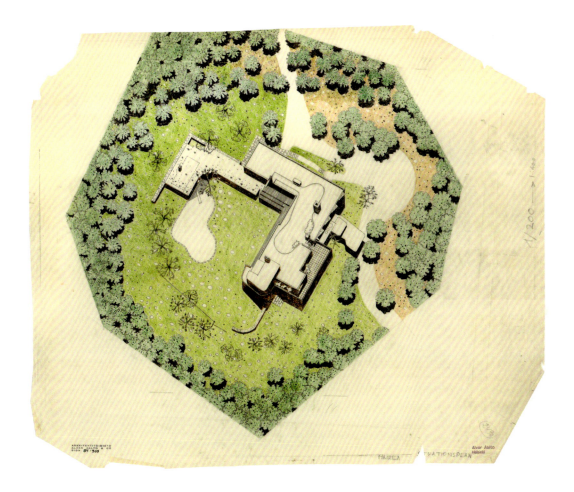

the garden as a covered terrace with a concrete frame holding up a grassed roof. This loggia structure joins with a sauna, enclosed by a low stone wall that returns to partially enclose the garden. The sauna, formed in timber, looks for all the world like it has been transported intact from ancient Japan. A small, roughly triangular deck from the sauna links to a small kidney-bean shaped pool.

Upstairs, the landing offers another space to sit, with a sinuous fireplace placed in one corner. The master bedrooms (his and hers, paired around a central en suite bathroom) lie above the large open-plan reception room, set back to provide an east-facing balcony. Maire's studio is tucked away in the corner, projecting out over the winter garden to form an angled, curved form. Children's bedrooms complete the frontage and open into a large play space, while guest rooms are arranged single-banked to occupy the return leg of the plan looking north-east into the forest. Full-height cupboards line the corridor to present a blank wall to the family's private garden.

The interior of the villa is a constantly changing palette of materials, colours and spatial experience – no white International Style space here, rather an array of timber floors and ceilings, tiles, carpet, rendered and painted brick, timber poles and rattan wrappings. Perhaps this constant invention is best represented by the various handles Aalto designed throughout the house: the front door has a bronze handle that angles to recall the sections of tree branches used traditionally on vernacular buildings, while within, handles appear in various guises, some with leather wrappings. The intensity of invention brings Pierre Chareau's Dalsace House to mind.

Externally, the changing material palette and invention continues. Approaching the house from the east it appears as a two-storey, lime-washed brick frontage. To the south side a large projecting form with a slate base gives way to timber windows, with a central bay infilled in fine horizontally slatted teak, capped by a vertically slatted teak-enclosed balcony. To the north side, beyond the curvy, dark-stained timber entrance canopy held up on clusters of timber poles, four upper-floor timber windows of the children's bedrooms project out as triangular oriels, angling back towards the sun.

Within the loosely defined courtyard garden, it is Maire's studio at first floor that turns the corner with a tall, dark-stained, vertically boarded blank wall. With rounded corners and a lower projecting balcony supported by a paired column, one of its sides is canted (and structurally redundant) above a distinctly Japanese screen into the winter garden. Again, the upper floor continues as a lime-washed brick with only two small openings (one into the upstairs landing, the other a doorway opening out to the terrace above the dining room), while the dining room projects out in white brick, terminated by a sudden blue-glazed tiled corner where a stone stair climbs up to the terrace enclosed by small-diameter horizontal tree trunks, stripped of bark and supported by steel uprights. This overt reference to the vernacular is continued in the turf-covered loggia and the sauna building. Overall, the effect of all the changes in materials is not only recognisably vernacular, but also painterly (Aalto was a very gifted painter), as if the blue tiles and the angled supports are touches that provide balance to a perfect composition. With so many allusions to nature, from twin-stemmed birch trees to the irregular, forest-like column spacings, to bamboo plantations and screens – even the curious moulding to one edge of the main fireplace where it meets the window, known in the office at the time as 'Aalto's ear', brings to mind the forms of wind-sculpted snow, as if melting by the fire – the house alludes to the organic. A final delicate touch perhaps acts as a suitable

VILLA MAIREA, NOORMARKKU, FINLAND

ABOVE:
The living room and stairs of Villa Mairea

metaphor for Aalto's architecture here, with a low ha-ha implying, rather than enclosing the courtyard, the open sides acting as a demarcation between the domestic realm and the forest: man and nature making peace with each other.

By 1939, with the villa receiving praise around the world (Sigfried Giedion famously likened it to 'architectural chamber music'), Aalto was at last secure, with fame and the work that followed. Cruelly, events around the world were to intervene again. With the USSR signing a non-aggression pact with Germany that year, it threatened Finland before finally invading the country on 30 November. Aalto avoided mobilisation and fled with his family to neutral Sweden. Orders followed him to Stockholm, where he faced a choice of returning for national service or a charge of desertion. He returned to Finland and was signed up as a second lieutenant but, before he saw action, he learnt that his brother Einar had taken his own life after being ordered to the front. Aalto used his connections to get himself transferred to a safe government job back in Helsinki. Again using

Exterior view of the garden and pool of Villa Mairea

his guile, he persuaded his superiors at the Government Information Centre that his skills would better serve the cause if he were to embark on a fundraising tour of America and so, in March 1940, with his wife and child, he left for New York. By the time he arrived in the United States, a Peace Treaty had been signed between Finland and the USSR, but by then thousands of Finns had lost their lives, including three of Aalto's young assistants. Harry Gullichsen had served throughout and survived. After seven months in the United States, Aalto had charmed his way to endless parties and even managed to gain a professorship at Massachusetts Institute of Technology (MIT), but finally he received a telegram from the Finnish Embassy stating, 'Res. 2nd lieutenant Aalto ordered to return to his post'. With the threat of military action reduced at home, the family returned in November 1940.

By May 1941 Finland was dragged back to war with the USSR. Aalto stayed at his job with the Government Information Centre and was promoted to lieutenant, while also running his practice. In the summer of 1943, Albert Speer, Hitler's architect, invited Aalto to visit Nazi Germany to see the progress they were making on standardised buildings. Although initially avoiding the invitation, he acquiesced when Speer sent a plane to Helsinki to fetch him. Back in Finland the Ahlström commissions kept coming, until war was finally over.

Many of Aalto's fellow countrymen were less than impressed by his wartime record, as summed up by Eeva Viljo, who was to contrast his friend Hahl's heroism and death on the front to Aalto's 'almost hysterical concern for his own safety and his shirking of wartime military assignments'. But although Aalto may not have been a wartime hero, by 1945 at the age of 47 he was hailed as the leading architect in Scandinavia, with an international reputation, an American professorship and a busy practice. Aino took up the reins of the office, in addition to managing the Artek company and the raising of their two children, supporting Aalto and keeping a check on his narcissism as he began to shuttle back and forth to MIT. He was regularly unfaithful, but it seems she tolerated this; as Viola Markelius had recalled 16 years previously, 'Sometimes we'd swap husbands, modern, liberated women that we were, and I must say that Aalto was a wonderful lover, my goodness!'

In 1946 Aino fell ill with breast cancer (she had had a successful operation for the same condition 15 years earlier) and she was to die at home on 13 January 1949. Aalto, who had lost his mother when he was just eight years old, once again lost his compass and threw himself into work, travel and, this time, hit the bottle. In 1950, he fell in love with another young assistant, 23 years his junior – Elsa Mäkiniemi (Elissa as Aalto christened her). They married in 1952 and lived and worked together for the rest of Aalto's life. Aalto continued to work, travel and drink hard until his death from a heart attack on 11 May 1976, aged 78.

The Villa Mairea stays in the Ahlström family and regularly opens to the public. As T.S. Eliot wrote, 'Meaningful buildings arise from tradition and they constitute and continue tradition. No architect worthy of his craft works alone; he works with the entire history of architecture in his bones.'

THE DESERT HOUSE,
PALM SPRINGS, CALIFORNIA, USA

Richard Neutra, 1946

WHEN EDGAR KAUFMANN, the department store magnate from Pittsburgh and owner of Frank Lloyd Wright's Fallingwater, decided to build a holiday home in California, he chose Wright's former assistant Richard Neutra as his architect. This infuriated the vainglorious Wright, who was by then in his late seventies.

Richard Joseph Neutra (known by friends and family as 'RJN') had arrived in America on 24 October 1923 on the SS *Laconia* from Hamburg. Born in Vienna in 1892, the fourth child of Samuel and Elizabeth Neutra, who had arrived in Austria from Hungary and Moravia respectively, he was to spend his first 28 years in Vienna, which was then the centre of European avant-garde culture. As a young man with flowing locks and good looks, Neutra was a ladies' man and, with his schoolfriend Ernst, the son of Sigmund Freud, he enjoyed a Bohemian lifestyle. This was threatened when one of his lovers, the 19-year-old Threska Sturm, became pregnant, but she had an abortion, after which they continued their affair until Neutra left Vienna.

Neutra was to write that he had found a calling to architecture at the age of eight while riding around the new Viennese subway with its startling stations designed by Otto Wagner. He joined the Imperial Institute of Technology, graduating in 1910 after which he served his obligatory year of military service. Returning to his studies in 1912, they were again interrupted two years later with the outbreak of war, when he was called to active duty as a reserve lieutenant. Neutra's military service ended with his becoming sick with malaria for two years before finally being hospitalised. He returned to complete his studies in 1917. On a sketching trip to Neuchatel in Switzerland two years later while staying in a boarding house of the Niedermann family, he met the 19-year-old Dione Niedermann, a talented musician, and fell in love. Over the next couple of years they spent a great deal of time apart as Neutra moved around Europe in search of work, finally ending up in the office of Erich Mendelsohn in Berlin. They got married in 1922.

Like Robert van't Hoff before him, having seen the Wasmuth Edition of Frank Lloyd Wright's work in 1914, Neutra had set his sights on going to America, where his friend from the Institute, Rudolph Schindler, was working in Wright's office. Determined to meet his hero Wright, he applied for a visa, but his applications were rejected for over three years until a peace treaty was signed

THE DESERT HOUSE, PALM SPRINGS, CALIFORNIA, USA

between America and Austria in August 1923. When Neutra finally arrived in America, he took work where could find it and settled for a while in the office of Holabird and Roche in Chicago. There he met another idol, Louis Sullivan, who died shortly afterwards, giving Neutra the opportunity to meet Wright at Sullivan's funeral. Neutra was to write of this first meeting that Wright 'was well dressed, carried a cane, and wore Oxfords with fairly high heels . . . he has the head of a lion resting on a somewhat well-proportioned body'.

Neutra went on to work for Wright at Taliesin in Wisconsin, arriving in the summer of 1924. Dione arrived in the autumn with their young son, named Frank after the great man. Having found his way to Taliesin after years of struggle, ambition soon called and he and Dione decided with some regret to move on and join Schindler, who had settled in California while running Wright's projects there.

Staying with Schindler and his wife Pauline in the house Schindler had designed in West Hollywood, Neutra began another long search for work. His breakthrough came with an apartment block he designed for J.H. Miller, whom he had met at a party. After the developer's finances failed and he skipped town to avoid his creditors, the building was finally realised in reduced form and was named the Jardinette Apartments. It was to catch the eye of the architectural critic Henry Russell Hitchcock, who commented in the *Architectural Record* that Neutra's apartments were 'as fine and as modern as any of this German work'.

In 1928, Neutra started to turn the corner with his first masterpiece – the Lovell Health House. He had met Philip and Leah Lovell through Schindler, as Leah's sister was a client of Wright's. In fact, Schindler had already built a house for the Lovells in 1926 – the Lovell Beach House – that was to become one of the landmarks of early modern architecture in California. But the job had left tension due to Schindler's apparent disregard for providing drawings on time and budget – not to mention his infatuation with Lovell's wife Leah.

Lovell was a practising 'naturopath', an anti-drug physician (now known as a homeopath). The Health House was to be a demonstration of health and the future: set on a spectacular and steep site in the Hollywood Hills, it was to have open

BELOW:
Richard Neutra and Rudolph Schindler, with Richard's wife Dione and their second son, Dion, *c.*1925

99

sleeping porches, private spaces for nude sunbathing and bathing areas for therapeutic needs. With this project, Neutra built the first steel-framed house in America, perhaps in homage to Sullivan and the Chicago School. Completed in 1929, Lovell, keen to promote the health aspects of his new home and convinced that, despite its large budget, it would offer many lessons for the most modest house, advertised a series of open days. An overwhelming 15,000 Los Angelenos turned up over four days and poured through the house, and it became a major local news item that spread across America. Neutra was suddenly famous and lauded as the next great American architect, arousing some resentment from Schindler. In 1932, Hitchcock declared in a commentary of an exhibition that included both Schindler's and Neutra's work that Schindler was a 'flawed and parochial Wrightian', whereas Neutra was 'the leading Modern architect of the West Coast'. During the following decade, Neutra received over 100 commissions and built over 50 buildings. He and Schindler lost touch.

In 1945, when Kaufmann appointed Neutra for his west coast home, he was in many ways anointing the new king. The site, at 470 West Vista Chino, lay on the edge of Palm Springs where the desert meets the San Jacinto Mountains. The 65 x 100 m (200 x 300 ft) plot offered a rugged desert landscape that Neutra likened to the imagined landscape of the moon. His plan for the house owed

ABOVE:
Richard Neutra's
Lovell Health House,
Los Angeles, 1929

OPPOSITE:
The Desert House
from the street

THE DESERT HOUSE, PALM SPRINGS, CALIFORNIA, USA

much to Wright and also perhaps to the memory of Mies van der Rohe's Country House plan – a pinwheel arrangement of single-storey wings with a living area at the hub and central stack of masonry signalling hearth as home.

A gated entrance for cars off the street is separated by a pile of giant boulders from a small pedestrian gate to one side, and a covered path along the back of a car port leads to the entrance lobby. This in turn opens directly into the central living space that Neutra called his 'public square'. With light grey polished concrete flooring and a white ceiling, the living area appears as a not unfamiliar International Style space, but a timber-boarded ceiling above the dining area immediately changes the nature of the space into something more in touch with natural materials, while the full-height glazed enclosure brings nature inside. A central fireplace in neatly chiselled Utah stone, laid with narrow, open joints (the mortar deeply recessed), was crafted by the same masons who had worked on Wright's Fallingwater nearly ten years earlier. The precision of the stonework lends an abstract feel to the heart of the house, neatly emphasising

the distance from Wright, in that his building was 'made, not grown'; it had been inserted into the landscape.

Rather than the white interiors that Neutra had used in earlier projects, the internal colours are rose, green, canary yellow and salmon, all set against white and the dark, neutral brown used to make certain walls appear to recede behind others. The glazing not only provides an elegant and minimal enclosure but, when opened, also disappears completely at the south-west corner of the room. The building suddenly seems to be merely a shelter from the sun, with no boundary between indoor and outdoor spaces. Drawing on Neutra's appreciation of Japanese architecture, it is this connection to nature that sets the Desert House apart: fusing European International Style and Wright's organic architecture, it combines into something unique in its time.

To realise such an elegant and seemingly weightless structure, Neutra employed a slender steel framework. He was fond of referring to the implausibly slim columns as 'spider legs', infilled with timber, much as Charles Gwathmey was to use on his own house some 19 years later. A gallery slides along the north side of the dining space and chimney where the Kaufmann's art collection, including Picassos and Cézannes, hung on a timber-clad wall. This leads to the master bedroom suite at the far end of the eastern wing that again has full-height glazing on two sides, with an open corner looking out onto a blue swimming pool. A solid stone wall runs along the back of the space and extends out as a garden wall before finally terminating with a garden store.

To the north of the 'public square', two large guest suites are connected by a broad covered deck, or 'breezeway', in which full-height vertical and rotating aluminium fins close off the west side to provide a windbreak, while a narrow lily pond adds thermal cooling to aid the prevailing breezes. To the west lies the wing containing the kitchen and staff accommodation. A fourth wing runs southwards, backing onto the entrance path and terminating with a large car port.

The cruciform, or pinwheel plan, with four wings stretching out into the landscape to the four points of the compass, ensures that every part of the house has not only its own sense of privacy, but each engages profoundly with the site and with nature. The four wings spin off the central living space, each shifted slightly so that it has a sense of spiralling, with the swimming pool located south

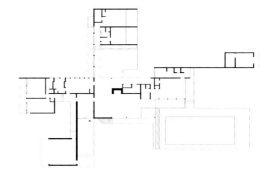

ABOVE:
Plan of the Desert House

OPPOSITE:
Interior view of the Desert House

of the living wing acting as the stabiliser to the composition. While the arms of the pinwheel ensure daylight and natural ventilation, the hot days of winter in Palm Springs yield to cold nights, so Neutra provided underfloor heating and this extended outdoors, right up to the pool to give warm toes to brave bathers.

Seen from outside, the house appears as a series of shimmering roof planes, each edged in subtly crimped metal, floating above expansive glazed screens, and this is counterpointed by the stone chimney rising up through the horizontals, pinning the whole edifice to the site. Above the living space and entrance hallway an open room crowns the house. This is the 'Gloriette' that Neutra remembered from the Schönbrunn Palace in Vienna – a 'little glory', a pavilion that has no walls, save a series of aluminium vertical louvres that adjust to provide shelter from the prevailing north-westerly desert winds. This neatly got around the planning restrictions that prohibited two-storey buildings and, in turn, gave the house a space that truly modified the climate in a passive way.

Neutra designed the garden using the principles of the 'natural garden' he had learnt from his mentor back in Europe, the Swiss landscape architect Gustav Ammann, who had 'intensified my understanding that architecture was a production intimately interwoven with nature and the landscape in which it was inserted'. Joshua trees, organ pipe cacti, agaves and large rocks provide a curious domesticity to the immediate environment of the house.

The house was built by the contractor 'Red' Marsh, who was to build many of Neutra's houses, and, at the insistence of Kaufmann, he used three crews, working 24 hours a day. Kaufmann kept a personal representative on the site and issued over 600 change orders. A house originally priced at $35,000 in the years immediately following the Second World War was to balloon to $295,000.

In 1947, the photographer Julius Shulman was to immortalise the house in a single photograph. Taken at dusk, with Liliane reclining by the pool with a bright light behind her, it perfectly captured the promise of outdoor living – sun chairs, pool, mountains and a house that hovered above its site, with walls

THE DESERT HOUSE, PALM SPRINGS, CALIFORNIA, USA

OPPOSITE:
Exterior view of the side elevation of the Desert House, with pool

ABOVE:
Frank Lloyd Wright's perspective drawing for an unbuilt house commissioned by Liliane Kaufmann in 1950

dissolving into nothing. The photograph made the pages of *Time* magazine in August 1949, with Neutra's portrait on the cover – completing his displacement of Wright as America's 'greatest living architect'. The text that accompanied the article provided a prescient summary of Neutra's influence on architecture in the United States: 'If what is now called "modern" eventually becomes traditional in the U.S., it will be not merely because more & more people have learned to like it. Modern architects will have been learning too, merging clean lines, common-sense convenience and liberating openness of style with the warm overtones of home.'

Some four years after the house was completed, Liliane's long-suffering patience with her husband's philandering broke and she left Edgar. In a mischievous twist, she employed Wright to design her own home on a nearby site. In a grand perspective drawing by Wright, his design for a large sinuous house has a dismissive little Desert House appearing at the top of the drawing, like an afterthought. Liliane died before the house could be built.

After Edgar Kaufmann died in 1955 the house lay empty for several years until it was sold, changing hands twice and enduring a 2200 sq ft extension by the architect William Cody in the 1960s, before it was sold on again in 1968 and then sold again to the singer Barry Manilow, who lived there from 1973 until 1992. It was then bought by Brent and Beth Harris – he was a successful investment manager and she an art historian – for $1.5 million. Horrified at the Laura Ashley wallpaper, marble-lined walls and rooftop air conditioning units, as well as the extensive additions and alterations, they employed the architects Leo Marmol and Ron Radziner to totally restore the house to its former glory.

EAMES HOUSE, PACIFIC PALISADES, CALIFORNIA, USA

Charles and Ray Eames, 1949

IN 1941, SHORTLY AFTER DIVORCING his first wife Catherine Woermann, whom he had married in 1929, Charles Eames wrote a wonderfully romantic, handwritten letter to the 29-year-old student Bernice 'Ray' Kaiser:

> Dear Miss Kaiser, I am 34 (almost) years old, single (again) and broke – I love you very much and would like to marry you very very soon* I cannot promise to support us very well but if given the chance will shure [*sic*] in hell try.
> * soon means very soon. Charlie.

Charles Ormond Eames Jr was head of the industrial design department at the Cranbrook Academy in Michigan and had met young Miss Kaiser, who was studying painting there, when she was brought in to help prepare drawings for Eames and his friend Eero Saarinen's submission for a furniture design competition held by the Museum of Modern Art (that they went on to win). She was an impish, petite woman and a talented artist with a zest for life, perhaps nurtured by her father's work at the Grand Theatre in Sacramento where she was raised. Given the pet name 'Ray-Ray' at home, she was to be known all her life as Ray. Within a month of Charles's divorce, the couple were married in Chicago and honeymooned by driving a new Ford across to California. With their marriage, a truly remarkable union of equal talents was founded. They were to become the most respected and successful couple in a wide range of design: architecture, industrial design, textiles, film, photography and furniture.

Settling in Los Angeles, Charles quickly found a job with MGM Studios, working in the art department. Ray met John Entenza, the publisher and editor of *Arts & Architecture*, who was to become something of a mentor and a lifelong friend to the couple, and she began designing covers for his magazine. Through Entenza the Eameses met Richard Neutra and were able to move into his recently completed Stathmore apartment building in the Westwood district of Los Angeles where they lived from 1941. At home, with their shared creativity and ceaseless interest in product design, the Eameses began to develop and test moulded plywood furniture in a spare room. By 1942, Charles took a leave of absence from MGM to work on a design for moulded-wood splints for the US navy – the war was by that time in full swing. Setting up their

EAMES HOUSE, PACIFIC PALISADES, CALIFORNIA, USA

PREVIOUS SPREAD:
Julius Shulman's photograph of Charles and Ray Eames sitting in the living room of Eames House in 1958

RIGHT:
Charles and Ray Eames in 1946

'Plyformed Wood Company', they manufactured a trial run of 5,000 splints and began developing stretchers and glider shells that resulted in government contracts. They took on premises at 901 Washington Boulevard in the Venice neighbourhood of Los Angeles that were to be the epicentre of their fertile minds. '901' as it became known, became an experimental research base, exploring a wide range of interests – with Charles a natural communicator who preferred images rather than words, and Ray who brought a painterly touch and faultless aesthetic judgement to all she laid hands on. In the sexual politics of 1950s America, Ray was always seen behind her husband and rarely spoke first, but to all who knew them she was an independent woman who called the shots. She had a penchant for wearing short-sleeved blouses and bohemian flared skirts that led to her being described as 'a delicious

109

LEFT:
Perspective sketch of Charles Eames and Eero Saarinen's unbuilt Bridge House (Case Study House 8), 1945

RIGHT:
Charles and Ray Eames standing on a steel frame in 1948

dumpling, in a doll's dress'. Charles was a good-looking man, casually dressed in open necked shirts and loose trousers. Their image as a very fashionable couple was to serve them well.

The Eameses began developing a series of experimental furniture pieces using plywood, plastic, fibreglass, wire mesh and aluminium. They made chairs, tables and storage units. Through commissions for the Herman Miller company that were launched under the slogan, 'We want to make the best, for the most, for the least', they were to become the most successful furniture designers of the 20th century.

In January 1945, Entenza launched the 'Case Study House Program' in the pages of *Arts & Architecture* magazine, which ran intermittently from 1945 to 1966. The scheme sought new ways to build inexpensive and efficient model homes for the US housing boom caused by the end of the Second World War and the return of millions of soldiers. It epitomised the optimism of the 1950s when the United States was at the height of its political and economic power, and its stated aim was that 'each house must be capable of duplication and in no sense be an individual performance'. 'It is important that the best material available be used in the best possible way in order to arrive at a "good" solution of each problem, which in the overall program will be general enough to be

EAMES HOUSE, PACIFIC PALISADES, CALIFORNIA, USA

of practical assistance to the average American in search of a home in which he can afford to live.' *Arts & Architecture* was to publish 36 designs, and 24 were realised. Entenza sponsored the houses through materials donated by industry and manufacturers, in return for extensive publicity, and the owners had to agree to open their houses to the public for eight weeks after completion.

Entenza owned a 2-hectare (5-acre) site on the bluff above the Pacific Coast Highway in the Pacific Palisades neighbourhood of Los Angeles, and with 0.8 hectares (2 acres) set aside for houses by Rodney Walker and Richard Neutra, he retained a 1.2-hectare (3-acre) meadow with many mature eucalyptus trees and commissioned Charles to design two houses with Saarinen, one for the Eameses – Case Study House 8 – and the other for Entenza – Case Study House 9. The designs appeared in *Arts & Architecture* in December 1945, with the Eameses' house as a bridge-like structure, perched at one end on the rising ground, and raised up and cantilevered on two columns, and Entenza's house as a single-storey structure.

Following on from Neutra's Desert House, which had been completed in 1946, the Eameses continued his use of a steel frame as the basis for their house.

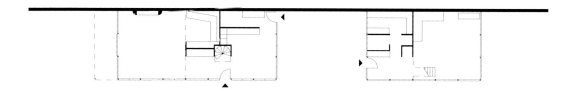

ABOVE:
Plan of
Eames House

RIGHT:
Exterior view of
Eames House

However, with their interest in industrial production – and industrial components – the house was to be the first that really elevated these components into a palette for domestic architecture. The house looks and feels bolted together, assembled from a kit of parts, rather than just built.

With the steel frame ordered but delayed due to material shortages, Charles and Ray redesigned their house, turning it by 90 degrees to align with the bank at the rear of the site, where they were to build a 57 m (175 ft) long, 2.4 m (8 ft) high retaining wall. This alignment was roughly east–west but had the benefit of allowing all the trees to remain on the site. With the steelwork finally turning up over two years later in 1948, they modified the components to construct two simple 5.2 m (17 ft) high frames, like a long warehouse. These had 10 cm (4 in) 'H' section columns at 2.2 m (7 ft 4 in) spacings, eight to form the house, with a gap of four bays for a central courtyard, then a further five bays for their studio. With a width equal to three bays, the resultant volumes were 15.5 x 6.6 m (51 ft x 22 ft 6 in) wide for the house, and 11.3 x 6.6 m (37 ft x 22 ft 6 in) for the studio. Horizontal lattice beams provided a roof and mezzanine floor to both spaces. The roof deck is in a ribbed steel decking that is exposed within. Industrial glazing systems painted a dark grey form the enclosure with infill panels in clear, translucent and wired glass, as well as large solid panels formed in steel sheeting finished externally in painted render.

On the south facade, the glazed bays are generally split into two panels and subdivided vertically into six, lending a horizontal quality that recalls traditional Japanese architecture. Two large planes, one to the upper level of the double-height living space, the other to the mezzanine landing, are painted white and bright blue respectively, while a third, a large black-painted panel, slightly recessed at the ground floor, marks the foot of the staircase and has a bold 'X' metal rod structural bracing. A single glazed panel in red balances the composition like a Piet Mondrian painting and brings Gerrit Rietveld's Schröder House to mind. The studio repeats the same elevational composition, with a solid white panel demarking the lower floor of the mezzanine space.

EAMES HOUSE, PACIFIC PALISADES, CALIFORNIA, USA

The main living room, a double-height space, is perfectly square in plan and sits behind an open-ended bay that forms a sheltered outdoor space – the same double-height square space to the far end of the studio acts as a bookend. With house and studio both entered from this central open court, there is also entry into service space beneath the mezzanine. To the house, a kitchen and dining area occupy the first three structural bays, and a spiral staircase – painted steel with plywood treads – leads up to bedroom spaces, the master suite and another that opens out onto the upper space of the living room, in Corbusian fashion. Tucked under the mezzanine floor off the large double-height living room lies a built-in sofa making a snug, leaving the main space free for an ever-changing collection of furniture and artefacts. White floor tiles and white-painted mezzanine make for a neutral, almost abstract backdrop to the interior, with only the rear wall clad in timber boarding adding a natural touch.

Once again, the photographer Julius Shulman, who had so perfectly captured the essence of Neutra's Desert House just a few years previously, immortalised the house – and the Eameses – in a single frame, with Charles and Ray sitting centrally. The photograph dates from 1958, nine years after the completion of the house. Charles sits on a curious high-backed, ankle-height

TWENTY GREAT HOUSES OF THE TWENTIETH CENTURY

chair, Ray to his right, sitting slightly lower. Charles is smiling and looking for all the world like an actor straight out of a Hollywood western. Ray her hands clasping her knees, stares straight at Charles in devotion, looking diminutive in such a big space neatly cluttered with rugs, cushions (no two alike), candelabras, carved wooden pieces, Ray's artworks, plants and their own furniture. In the foreground is their 1956 Lounge Chair and Ottoman – the most iconic of all their furniture. This was an assemblage of rosewood curved plywood shells, luxurious buttoned back leather filled with foam, down and duck feathers, all elevated on cast aluminium 'spider' mechanisms. A ladder attached to the roof beam provides access to hang artworks, as well as a piece of tumbleweed sitting top right of the upper gallery that the Eameses had collected on their honeymoon. This photograph shows the house as a place of a constantly changing collage and an experiment in living.

Charles was to describe the house as 'unselfconscious'. In making a house specifically to meet their needs, they realised the needs of all humans. Upon completion, the house was ahead of its time and was to prove highly influential. The Eameses went on to complete Entenza's house next door, and in 1954 the De Pree House, but neither could surpass their own home. It proved

Exterior view of Eames House

that industrial components could make a container for living a good life. A generation later, the architects of the British 'high-tech' movement would extend the Eameses' tenets to encompass sleek office buildings, airports and cultural centres.

The Eameses lived out their lives in the house, and with 901 attracting clients such as Boeing, IBM, and Polaroid, they became the Apple of their day. With such success came enormous pressure and Charles considered throwing it all in towards the end. He betrayed his beloved Ray by chasing the young art historian Judith Wechsler, declaring that he would leave Ray and the Eames office to run away and marry her, but Wechsler rebuffed his proposal out of loyalty to Ray. Ray was of course deeply hurt, but they carried on, with Ray outliving Charles by exactly ten years – they both died on 24 August, he of a heart attack while on a lecture tour in St Louis in 1978, she of cancer in 1988.

Charles's daughter Lucia from his first marriage established the Eames foundation to preserve the house and offer an educational experience. The house was named a National Historic Landmark and placed on the National Register of Historic Places in 2006. The house is today open to tours, and with most of the interiors roped off the visitor is presented with a tableau full of the couple's possessions, making their absence beyond poignant.

> Make a list of books
> Develop a curiosity
> Look at things as though for the first time
> Think of things in relation to each other
> Always think of the next larger thing
> Avoid the 'pat' answer – the formula
> Avoid the preconceived idea . . .
> The art is not something you apply to your work
> The art is the way you do your work, a result of your attitude towards it
> Charles Eames's notes on advice to students, January 1949

FARNSWORTH HOUSE, FOX RIVER, ILLINOIS, USA

Mies van der Rohe, 1951

DR EDITH FARNSWORTH WAS A SMART 42-year-old doctor, a kidney specialist who also held a degree in English Literature and Composition from the University of Chicago. In 1945, with a plan to build a modest country retreat, she purchased 3.6 hectares (9 acres) of an old farmstead on the banks of the Fox River, in Plano, some 100 km (60 miles) south-west of Chicago. At some point later that year, she met Mies van der Rohe at a small dinner party. She recalled this moment years later, 'One evening I went to have dinner with Georgia [Lingafelt] and Ruth [Lee] in their pleasant old-fashioned apartment in the Irving. Also invited that evening was the massive stranger whom Georgia, with her peculiarly sweet smile, introduced, as I slipped off my coat: This is Mies, darling.'

Mies had been in the United States since he had left Berlin under the shadow of fascism in 1938 to head the architecture department at the Illinois Institute of Technology. With the war now over, Mies had no intention of returning to Europe and, with his international reputation, his practice in Chicago was burgeoning. He was 59 when he met Edith Farnsworth and she was a single, middle-aged woman; by all accounts not a beauty, rather tall and with equine features, but with an attractive and powerful intellect. She described in her memoirs the meeting with Mies and how she talked of her recent acquisition and hopes to build a small retreat there, and how after some two hours with the famously taciturn architect, he came out with, 'I would love to build any kind of house for you'. 'The effect was tremendous, like a storm, a flood, or other act of God', she recalled, sounding somewhat awestruck in the presence of the great man.

BELOW:
Mies van der Rohe in c.1965

In the years since, there have been rumours that the two had an affair. Farnsworth's sister Marion Carpenter was later to recall in an interview that Edith 'was mesmerized by him and she probably had an affair with him'. The truth has proved so far impossible to know, although a new Hollywood movie with Ralph Fiennes playing the Teutonic architect and Maggie Gyllenhaal as Dr Farnsworth may well turn this into the stuff of legend. What is known is that they were to fall out in

FARNSWORTH HOUSE, FOX RIVER, ILLINOIS, USA

TOP:
Plan of Mies van der Rohe's unbuilt Country House, 1923

BOTTOM:
Edith Farnsworth in c.1940s

spectacular fashion. Whether it was Farnsworth's gripes about the cost overruns, the environmental failings, her private space being so exposed to passers-by – or a failed romance – remains a mystery. And was Mies not seeing his former lover, the sculptor Lora Marx, again? He had once said, 'I do not belong to anyone who doesn't know how to live alone'. His abandoned partner Lilly Reich back in Berlin and his former wife Ada would both recognise this quality in him.

By 1946, after several picnic trips together to the site, Mies was commissioned and started work. The brief was simple – a weekend retreat for a single person, so there was little need for privacy or the accumulation of possessions – and so allowed for the pursuit of the Platonic ideal, a goal he had pursued for three decades. From his 1923 design for a Country House where space is captured rather than enclosed by walls, Mies had developed his ideas of open interiors. Partly realised through the Tugendhat House 21 years previously and through a series of unbuilt projects, they were to reach their zenith with the Farnsworth House.

The house is a glass pavilion, a white-painted steel frame raised up above the flood plain. It appears as three floating horizontal planes – terrace, floor and roof – almost magically suspended in the air. Eight supporting columns appear distinct as they are not only set in from the corners but are attached to

119

the outside edges of the planes, and stop short of the top, so the planes appear to be fixed as if by a magnetic force. Full-height glazed windows enclose the interior, leaving an open terrace to one end. Within this apparent simplicity lies much complexity, refined to the essence.

The entire house plan is based on the module of the fine 3 cm (1¼ in) thick Roman travertine slabs that cover inside and outside floors – these are 61 x 83 cm (2 ft x 2 ft 9 in) laid lengthwise along the house – so the house and terrace is 27 slabs long and 14 slabs wide or 22.4 x 8.54 m (74 x 28 ft) – a double square in plan. Mies, with his knowledge of stone from his father's carving workshop, surely chose Travertine to ground the uncompromising design associations with ancient Rome. The actual area of the house is a mere 135 sq m (*c.*1250 sq ft). The enclosed space occupies 19 slabs, so 15.8 m (52 in) long. The terrace suspended halfway from the ground is 19 slabs long by 11 wide, so 15.7 x 6.7 m (52 x 22 ft). The insistent use of the 61 x 83 cm (2 ft x 2 ft 9 in) slab module again connects the house back to history.

The columns are spaced eight slabs apart, or 6.6 m (21 ft), and are chunky 20 cm (8 in) square 'I' sections. The windows are on a four-slab module, so 3.32 m (11 ft) wide. In section, the house is raised up 157 cm (5 ft 3 in) above the ground to deal with seasonal flooding of the Fox River. Channels 38 cm (15 in) deep form the edges of the terrace, floor and roof, and with the flanges facing inward to receive precast concrete floor slabs, present a smooth face to the exterior. Floor and roof are separated by 2.9 m (9 ft 6½ in) – the height of the glazing. With the columns set back from the outer edges 1.5 m (5 ft) at each end and welded to the channels, the effect of the horizontal planes seemingly sliding past the verticals is complete. With the columns terminating a few inches below the roof, a steel angle projects out 5 cm (2 in) to cap the edifice. The terrace, located on the southern side, sits to the west and creates a second rectangle on plan – both united by five broad stone steps that seem to float in the air.

With this structure employing welded connections for the first time in his work, Mies united structure and architecture into a harmonious order resulting in a Platonic whole. It is apt that this plan should appear from his office in nearby Chicago, the city that mastered the steel frame with the Chicago School architects of the 19th century. It lays a long way from Corbusier's 1914 Dom-ino frame of six columns and three floors that was

ABOVE:
Plan of Farnsworth House

OPPOSITE:
Exterior view of Farnsworth House in autumn

FARNSWORTH HOUSE, FOX RIVER, ILLINOIS, USA

intended for mass production. For Mies the driving force was reduction, distilling eight columns and three floors to the absolute minimum, while keeping an eye on the classical tradition of proportion and harmony.

Within this beautiful, white, fully glazed frame, Mies continued his distillation of the elements by condensing all the paraphernalia of living – bathrooms, storage and utility/plant spaces – into a single rectangular form that sits off-centre within the space. This plywood-clad timber 'box' floats within the pavilion, stopping short of the ceiling – although a small section set well back from the periphery does connect to the roof for rainwater pipes and the like. It is like a giant piece of furniture, organising the space around it. The 2.4 m (8 ft) high Primavera panels have a warm, slightly orange glow and contrast sharply with the white-painted ceilings and cream stone floors, bringing a warmth, a domesticity, to the interior. By the positioning of this box, a narrow space to the north provides a galley kitchen, while a wider space to the south is the living area. A sleeping area is defined to the east, so that the rising sun can greet the sleeper each morning. Bathrooms, one for Dr Farnsworth and another for guests, are entered from the short sides and a utility room containing heating plant sits in the middle.

The space within the house was contemplative and serene but exposed to the landscape. In spring, the pavilion floated above a sea of daffodils, in summer above a verdant meadow, in autumn it sat within the gold of foliage and in winter it became at one with a carpet of snow. When the Fox River flooded, it floated like a houseboat.

A model closely resembling the final version of the house was exhibited at the Museum of Modern Art in New York in 1947, but Dr Farnsworth had to wait for an inheritance before work could start. Construction finally went ahead in September 1949 but by this time something had gone wrong between architect and client – the romance was over it seemed. A few months after meeting, the doctor had sent a handwritten letter to Mies: 'It is impossible to pay in money for what is made by heart and soul! Such work one can only recognize and cherish – with love and respect.' But years later she was to recall that, 'Perhaps as a man he is not the clairvoyant primitive that I thought he was, but simply colder and more cruel than anybody I have ever known. Perhaps it was never a friend and collaborator, so to speak, that he wanted, but a dupe and a victim.'

Upon completion, the house received rapt reviews. Architects and critics were amazed at the clarity and precision of the design, but the popular lay magazine *House Beautiful* berated it, calling it 'cold', 'barren' and 'sterile' – an example of the International Style that threatened traditional American values. Frank Lloyd Wright weighed in with 'The International Style . . . is totalitarianism. These Bauhaus architects ran from political totalitarianism in Germany to what is now made by specious promotion to seem their own totalitarianism in art here in America . . .'. This from a man who had admired Mies's work and regarded him as a friend in the 1930s and 1940s.

Dr Farnsworth wrote to Mies: 'I thought you could animate a predetermined, classic form like this with your own presence. I wanted to do something "meaningful", and all I got was this glib, false sophistication . . .'. In her memoirs, she remembered her first night at the house before it was fully completed in 1950:

> It was an uneasy night, partly from the novel exposure provided by the uncurtained glass walls and partly from the dread of Mies' implacable intentions. Expenses in connection with the house had risen far beyond what I had expected or could well afford and the glacial bleakness of that winter night showed very clearly how much more would have to be spent before the place could be made even remotely inhabitable.

So, whether it was the failed relationship, the cost overrun, the excessive condensation, freezing conditions in winter or the unbearably hot conditions in summer, it ended up in a bitter court hearing. It was Mies who took the doctor to court in 1953 for unpaid fees of $28,173. She countersued for $33,870, claiming that the architect had misrepresented the cost of the house to her, as

FARNSWORTH HOUSE, FOX RIVER, ILLINOIS, USA

Interior view of Farnsworth House

well as his abilities as an architect. After this bruising encounter, a settlement of $14,000 was awarded in Mies's favour. She had, after all, approved the plans and supervised the construction. Seeking justice, and perhaps revenge, the doctor lashed out in the press: 'The truth is that in this house with its four walls of glass I feel like a prowling animal, always on the alert. I am always restless. Even in the evening. I feel like a sentinel on guard day and night. I can rarely stretch out and relax . . .'

There is no doubt that the house was a critical triumph but, sadly for the doctor, it was also an environmental disaster. The roof was formed in thin precast concrete slabs with a mere 5 cm (2 in) of insulation above – crucially, the science of condensation was not understood in the 1940s and 1950s. Internal environments in houses get humid and moist, and when this air meets a cold surface, condensation results. This happened not only on the underside of the concrete to the roof (hidden above a suspended plastered ceiling, so its presence appeared stealthily, but insistently over time), but also across the

6 mm (¼ in) thick single glazing and solid-steel window frames that streamed down to collect on the floor. The floor was built in precast and *in situ* concrete with no insulation and, exposed underneath to the elements, despite the floor coils for underfloor heating, nothing could make this warm. In summer, the fully glazed walls and poor cross-ventilation, with no sun screening save the foliage of a few trees, allowed the interior to become oven-like and, as a final but inevitable challenge, clouds of mosquitos plagued the house on the banks of a river, as there were no insect screens.

Like Corbusier's Villa Savoye – the perfection of a white, Purist construction that evaporated with the first crack in the render and was destroyed by weathering – so the beguiling, polished white frame of the Farnsworth House was quickly diminished by rust spots. Ironically, it was Wright who defended Mies's leaking building to a client, saying, in a sheer masterclass in arrogance, 'This is what happens when you leave a work of art out in the rain'.

Perhaps the worst problem came from rises in the flood levels of the river – Mies had established a maximum flood level back in 1946 of about 90 cm (3 ft) but, as the nearby city burgeoned and paved over the earth, run-off increased dramatically in the 1950s. The first flood to engulf the house came three years after the doctor moved in in 1954, ruining carpets and furniture, although the timber core was repairable. In 1996 a deluge resulted in some of the glass walls breaking and this time destroying the timber core, causing over $500,000 worth of damage.

Despite the problems and Dr Farnsworth's rancour, she continued to live in the house for the next 20 years. She never furnished it properly and avoided visitors. When the county highways department decided to widen and realign the road and bridge along the western boundary of the site, requiring the compulsory purchase of a 60 m (200 ft) wide strip of land, there ensued another court battle – and another loss. The road was built in 1967 and the following year Dr Farnsworth put the house up for sale. In the 1970s she retired from practice and moved to Italy, where she finally found love with an Italian poet. She died near Florence in 1977, aged 74.

After a three-year illness with cancer of the oesophagus, Mies died in a Chicago hospital on 17 August 1969 at the age of 83. He was by then celebrated as one of the greatest architects of the 20th century. Despite its failings, the Farnsworth House had an enormous influence on architecture across the world. The first example of its influence was actually completed just before Farnsworth, by Mies's friend and disciple Philip Johnson. He was unapologetic in basing his design for his own Glass House on the 1947 model for the Farnsworth House. It remains inferior, but Johnson was a master of publicity and it is reported that Mies 'stormed out in a huff when he saw it'.

In 1972 a British property developer and devotee of Mies, Lord (Peter) Palumbo, bought the house from Dr Farnsworth, describing her as, 'a difficult, ferocious woman'. Palumbo entrusted the refurbishment of the house to Mies's grandson Dirk Lohan. A complete restoration took place, installing vapour barriers to control condensation, new waterproofing to the roof, new heating plant and the interior was entirely rebuilt. The problem with flooding remained, and even after spending over $1 million on the restoration, a solution was not found. Ideas for hydraulic jacks to raise the entire structure in case of flood were mooted, but the house remains on the flood plain at its original elevation. Thoughts to relocate the house entirely were also considered but, while the house could be lifted and placed elsewhere, or even in a museum, it is the relationship between the house and its site that is the essence of the work. Ironically, Mies's next house – the 1952 McCormick House in Elmhurst, Illinois – a close cousin of the Farnsworth house, a glass and steel pavilion that had a similar plan albeit with some solid walls and sat on the ground – was relocated after 22 years to a nearby park, where it became a local art museum.

In 2001 a private group in Illinois, the National Trust for Historic Preservation, purchased the once again pristine property from Palumbo for a little over $7.5 million. The house was designated a National Historic Landmark in 2006. It is now a visitor attraction. The house was flooded once again by the remnants of Hurricane Ike in September 2008, and once again renovated.

UTZON HOUSE, HELLEBÆK, DENMARK

Jørn Utzon, 1952

JØRN UTZON'S NAME HAS BECOME synonymous with the Sydney Opera House and the debacle that led him and his family to leave Sydney under a cloud fuelled by political change in 1966, never to return. Yet what he left was to become one of the most iconic buildings in the world – a building that is emblematic of the Australian nation. A world away, and some 14 years earlier, he had completed his own modest house in the small coastal town of Hellebæk, some 40 km (25 miles) north of Copenhagen. It was to become the most influential Scandinavian house of the age.

In 1933 the Danish government set up the State Loan Programme with the intention of helping lower-income families to build a home in the suburbs to alleviate the most overcrowded parts of Copenhagen, providing 85 per cent loans at a low interest rate over a 35-year term. The programme required the use of an architect and limited floorspace to 100 sq m (1075 sq ft), later changed to 130 sq m (1,400 sq ft). This spawned a rash of new, experimental low-cost houses, mainly single-storey and many built from the ubiquitous yellow brick that quickly gained acceptance for a new modern architecture across Denmark in the 1930s. After the war, the State Loan Programme allowed many young architects to build their own homes and, although founded on this, due to technical issues the programme ultimately did not include Jørn Utzon's own home in Hellebæk that was competed in 1952.

LEFT:
Jørn Utzon *c.*1955

UTZON HOUSE, HELLEBÆK, DENMARK

Utzon was born in Copenhagen in 1918, the son of the internationally recognised yacht designer, Aage Utzon. As a child his family moved to Alborg, where his father was director of a shipyard and the young Utzon helped out drawing up plans and models. His interest in art and his innate skill in drawing led one of his father's cousins, Einar Utzon-Frank, who was a sculptor and a professor at the Royal Academy of Fine Arts in Copenhagen, to provide additional inspiration. As a dyslexic, Utzon did not do well academically, but his talent for drawing was so strong that he gained acceptance into the Academy of Fine Arts in Copenhagen. He had met his future wife Lis Fenger in April 1940, on his 20th birthday and, as it happened, just as the Nazi stormtroopers arrived in Copenhagen. Upon graduation in 1942, Utzon married Lis and they left Denmark for neutral Sweden, where he worked briefly for the architect Hakon Ahlberg and later with Paul Hedquist, who continued Erik Gunnar Asplund's practice following his early death in 1954 at the age of 55. He remained in Sweden for the duration of the war, returning to Denmark briefly after the war, before going to Helsinki to work briefly in the office of Alvar Aalto.

After the war, Denmark's architectural culture was known as Skønvirke, the Arts and Crafts movement in Scandinavia. This had evolved out of ideas from England and from the work of Frank Lloyd Wright and his argument for an 'organic architecture' as well as a renewed interest in vernacular architecture. This had started with Asplund's own summerhouse in Stennäs, built in 1937 south of Stockholm, that was to prove a touchstone for the next generation of architects in Denmark. Perhaps the first major building from this period to encapsulate Skønvirke was the Grundtvig's Church in Copenhagen by Peder Jensen-Klint that was begun in 1921 but, after his death in 1930, was completed by his son Kaare Klint in 1940. Here the entire building was based on a standard yellow brick that determined the form and all its details, so fusing ancient traditions into something entirely new with expression derived wholly from the material used in its construction. Kaare Klint proved to be just as influential as his late father, founding the furniture department at the Royal Academy School of Architecture in

Jensen-Klint's Grundtvig's Church, Copenhagen, 1940

129

Copenhagen and so laying the foundation for modern Danish furniture design in 1924 and reinforcing the link between craft and architecture.

Utzon had developed a series of house designs during the 1950s, indebted to Wright's Usonian houses, so perhaps fittingly referred to as 'Utzonian houses', that extended but never equalled the Hellebæk house. It was the 1954 competition-winning design for low-cost housing in Skåne in southern Sweden that began to crystallise the next development of the language of domestic architecture. This was entered under the title 'Private Life' and a more suitable epigram for Utzon's approach to domestic life would be hard to find. This design marked not only the beginning of a lifelong exploration of the courtyard house form, but also an enduring fascination with the enclosing wall as the foundation of the domestic realm.

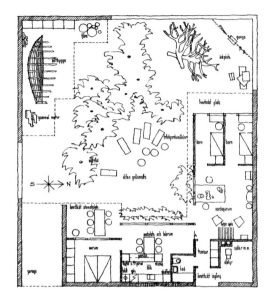

ABOVE:
Jørn Utzon's competition-winning 'Private Life' house plan, 1954

OPPOSITE:
Plan of Utzon House

The Utzons bought the plot of land in Hellebæk, a coastal town some 5 km (3 miles) north-west of Helsingor (home of Kronborg Castle, Shakespeare's Elsinore, the setting for *Hamlet*) and some 40 km (25 miles) north of Copenhagen. The land was acquired from a philosopher of religion who owned a large house with extensive grounds and the idea was that Utzon's nephew might take the adjacent plot. Utzon had even sketched out a possible full-size plan in the snow, but the idea fell through. Jørn and Lis camped on their site for several months to save money and ensure they chose the perfect spot for their new home. Eventually Utzon built a full-size model on the site using 2.5 x 5 m (8 x 16 ft) posters on canvas and wooden frames he begged from a nearby stadium following a six-day cycle race – his parents were invited to see the creation but the whole thing blew down before they got there. Utzon was to write that 'The simple, primitive life in the country; trips into the mountains with skis and guns, sailing trips, a few weeks together with Arabs in the mountains and the desert, a visit to North America and Mexico, the lifestyle of the Indians – all this has formed the basis for the way of life my wife and I have wanted to lead, and thus for the design of the house.'

The site is approached by a narrow track that rises slightly before dropping down into a shallow valley, crosses a local railway line and then turns before

UTZON HOUSE, HELLEBÆK, DENMARK

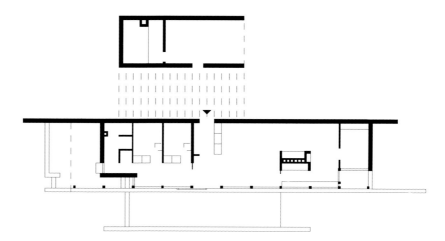

you arrive at the house. The building enigmatically appears at the last minute as a long blank wall with a pergola linking across to a garage set to one side. A single doorway provides the only break in the long, ochre-coloured brick wall. Utzon's response to the site is emphatic, throwing up the solid wall against the nearby tall fir trees and the north winds. Utzon wrote in 1989 that 'The wall, as protection and architectural element is something I have studied throughout the world, in China, Algeria, and in the Andes mountains. One can place small, delicate living things in front of it.'

The blank brick garage block contains space for a car and a small plant room. It was Utzon's studio and where the design for an international competition to build a new Opera House in Sydney, Australia, was carried out.

Once through the entrance door, it becomes clear that the house is in fact a timber construction that sits on a low, raised platform and rests against the unbroken brick wall, with the whole composition anchored by a large masonry fireplace. Arranged between the protective brick wall and a parallel 'open' wall to the south, all the living and sleeping spaces are arranged, sheltering beneath a boarded ceiling that sails out to provide shading to the glazing. The southern-facing wall is formed of broad, glazed screens – Utzon disliked Wright's close-spaced mullions on his houses – originally with low-level transoms that were later removed when larger sheets of glass became available. Beneath the roof

Exterior view of the front door of Utzon House

overhang, a brick terrace extends further out terminated by a parallel, low brick wall echoing the unbroken northern wall. The brick terraces extend each end into the landscape and step with the topography.

From the entrance lobby, a door opens into a single open-plan space of some 18 x 5.6 m (59 x 18 ft) – to one side lies the living space with a central brick fireplace that doubles up as part of a kitchen, while to the other is a children's play area and two bedrooms. A sliding screen set within one of the entrance lobby flank walls pulls out to separate the play area from the living space. Another smaller sliding screen could be pulled out of the fireplace wall to close the open end of the kitchen. The children's bedrooms are minimal, only as wide as a bed's length and just over 2.5 m (8 ft 4 in) deep, with one small cupboard each and both lit only by a single rooflight. Their daughter, Lin – destined to become one of Denmark's most celebrated artists and textile designers – spent years carefully whittling away the mortar in the brick wall in a bid for a tiny opening. Beyond the bedrooms lie a family bathroom and a doorway opening out onto a partially covered terrace to the westernmost end of the house. The parents' bedroom, only slightly larger and with full-height glazing, lies at the far end of the living space.

The interior of the house resonates with the traditional Japanese houses that Utzon had experienced first-hand at the Zui Ki tea house built in Stockholm in 1935. Underpinned by a module of 12 cm (a brick and joint) that dictated doors, cupboards and so on, walls and doors in Oregon pine extend from floor to

UTZON HOUSE, HELLEBÆK, DENMARK

ceiling, with black-painted strips at the top separating the vertical and horizontal planes. The ceilings are also formed in pine boards while floors are carpeted, save the areas of the entrance hall, and the yellow-brown tiles that are used on the kitchen floor and around the fireplace. Electric underfloor heating was used throughout (Utzon admired the Chinese tradition of heating below raised sections of floors).

With his spare use of brick, tile, timber and full-height glazing, Utzon galvanised a palette that would come to define Scandinavian modernism. It was to find its apotheosis in Wilhelm Wohlert and Jørgen Bo's Louisiana Museum of Modern Art in Humlebæk that opened to the public in 1958, bringing a domestic idiom to an institution. But it was Wohlert's exhibition house built in a large hall on the outskirts of Copenhagen, known as Huset i Haven (House and Garden), later also known as the Ønskehuset (Dream House), the following year, that would find its way into newspapers and onto television and was to really catch the public imagination.

While the Hellebæk house brings Wright's Usonian houses to mind with its flat-roofed, linear plan, closed back and open garden side, it also echoes the abstraction of Mies van der Rohe's Country House project and his German Pavilion in Barcelona, with the use of singular walls that extend from house to landscape, enclosing space between planes. Yet Utzon also fused his interest in ancient architecture, such as the use of platforms in Mayan structures and modular internal planning from traditional Japanese architecture, into his work.

Wilhelm Wohlert's Huset i Haven (House and Garden), later also known as the Ønskehuset (Dream House), Copenhagen, 1959

TWENTY GREAT HOUSES OF THE TWENTIETH CENTURY

TOP:
Exterior view of Utzon House

LEFT:
Interior view of Utzon House

134

UTZON HOUSE, HELLEBÆK, DENMARK

On 29 January 1957, with Jørn and Lis out on a morning walk to collect the post, the telephone rang and their daughter Lin, then ten years old, answered. With the news from the call, she rushed off to seek her parents and, upon finding them, threw her bicycle in a ditch and announced that daddy had won the Sydney Opera House competition, so now there was no excuse for not buying her the white horse she wanted. Life was never to be the same again for the family.

With the money from the Opera House commission, Utzon extended the house by building a parallel wing to the rear that was completed by 1959. While the extension is beautifully designed, it inevitably took much of the purity away from the modest original. In 1963 the Utzon family emigrated to Australia and rented the house out to friends. With his forced resignation from the Opera House commission in 1966, they returned to Europe and divided their time between Hellebæk and the Mediterranean island of Majorca, where Jørn and Lis were finally to settle in 1971.

The Hellebæk house remained largely empty during the 1980s and 1990s and, in 2004, it was passed on to their architect son Jan. It was listed by the Danish Agency for Culture in 2005. In this modest building, Utzon encapsulated what a modern house in Denmark should look like, and its influence remains pervasive to this day.

The Utzon family by the fireplace of Utzon House in c.1956

135

NIEMEYER HOUSE (CASA DAS CANOAS), RIO DE JANEIRO, BRAZIL

Oscar Niemeyer, 1953

OSCAR RIBEIRO DE ALMEIDA NIEMEYER SOARES FILHO not only had a poetically long name but also lived an enormously long life. Born seven years before the First World War, he finally died in 2012, 23 years after the invention of the World Wide Web, at the age of 104.

Known simply as Oscar, he was a true *Carioca*, a child of the city of Rio de Janeiro – his *cidade maravilhosa* (marvellous city). Born into a wealthy family, Niemeyer was raised into the colonial traditions of Brazil but, as he grew up, he became dissatisfied with the social injustices he saw around him in a society that was in transition as it began to wean itself off its dependency on Europe. It was to be Niemeyer who would revolt against the European academic-historical architecture and, later, against the rigid geometries of the International Style.

As a boy Niemeyer's first love was football, but he also loved to draw and was a natural, so at the age of 23 he joined Rio's Fine Arts Academy (an architecture course was not created until 1936) and graduated four years later in 1934. He initially worked at his father's typography business and then became an intern in the office of one of his tutors, Lúcio Costa, the spiritual father of Brazilian modernism. Born in France and educated in England, Switzerland and Brazil, Costa was a man of enormous erudition and sophistication. He was a champion of Corbusier's 'sacred book of architecture' (*Vers une architecture*). In the early 1930s he began a reform of the outmoded Beaux-Arts curriculum of the Academy. He brought in new blood committed to the ideals of the European avant-garde, while maintaining a respect for Brazilian traditions. Under Costa's generous wing, Niemeyer was brought into a team that was to work with the master himself, as the Minister of Education and Health under President Vargas invited Le Corbusier to come to Rio as a design consultant and to offer seminars on his work.

BELOW:
Oscar Niemeyer in front of the pool of Niemeyer House *c.* 1956

The impact of Corbusier on Niemeyer was to be instant and profound. He recalled years later his first meeting at the airport with the great man: 'He seemed to be an architect-genius come down from heaven. If, on the one hand, he was sometimes overly eager to make his own architecture, on the other hand I always felt he was a human being who carried a message, a paean to beauty that could not be silenced.'

In a six-week collaboration, Corbusier and a group of Brazilian architects that included Costa and Niemeyer produced the design for the Ministry of Education and Health building. This was destined to be the first major monument of the Modern Movement in South America and was completed in 1943. Corbusier was to praise Rio's 'unforgettable magic', falling under the influence of its dramatic topography, its festivals and its women. The trip coincided with his own turn away from 'white' architecture and his renewed interest in regional and deeper cultural connections, natural materials and organic forms.

The Ministry building carried the hallmarks of Corbusier's recent works in creating a large slab block lifted up on *pilotis*, like his Pavillon Suisse in Paris of 1931. While the Ministry had box-like forms, at ground level these gave way to more fluid plan arrangements. It seems that what impressed Niemeyer was witnessing Corbusier's spontaneous sketching, his improvisation and freedom of conceptualisation. This left an indelible impression on Niemeyer; it was the catalyst that released his talent. He awoke to the sensuous forms around him, the landscapes and, as he was always keen to point out, the curves of Brazilian women. He wrote, 'It is not the right angle that attracts me, nor the straight line, hard and inflexible, created by man. What attracts me is the free and sensual curve — the curve that I find in the mountains of my country, in the sinuous course of its rivers, in the body of the beloved woman.' He had found his path.

Niemeyer's first building to demonstrate this came with the Brazilian Pavilion at the 1939 World Fair in New York, again in collaboration with Costa. Corbusier's influence is clear with a *promenade architecturale* of ramps and *pilotis*, and a passing resemblance to his Pavillon de L'Esprit Nouveau of 1925, but the plan glories in sinuous curves. An angled ramp bends top and bottom as it rises up to an auditorium and viewing deck, with a sweeping aperture cut out of the roof above; an exhibition wing snakes back to one side above free-form walls defining information, coffee and even dance spaces. To the rear, the centrepiece is a serpentine lily pond and tropical garden. Overall, the building's rectilinear basic form becomes invaded, and counterpointed by fluid forms.

Niemeyer's first independent expression of free-form modernism came the following year when he was commissioned by the mayor of the city of Belo Horizonte to create something of a playground for the newly rich elite – a complex that included a leisure club, yacht club, dance hall and restaurant, a hotel and even a small chapel – all set around a lake. He let loose a riot of forms – meandering concrete canopies, parabolic vaults, twisting ramps. After this, he became something of a celebrity and clients queued at his door.

Niemeyer had married Annita Baldo, daughter of Italian immigrants from Padua, in 1928 and they had one child, Anna Maria, in 1930. In 1951 they bought a site high upon a forested hillside in Canoas, south-east of Rio. At the centre of the site was an enormous boulder that heaved up out of the ground to head height, so Niemeyer, echoing Frank Lloyd Wright at Fallingwater 14 years previously, made this outcrop the nexus of the design. To one side he placed the house and to the other, an oval-shaped pool.

LEFT:
Oscar Niemeyer's concept sketch of Niemeyer House

RIGHT:
Exterior view of Niemeyer House

The house appears as if a thin stratum of cloud, hovering over the site among the trees. This sinuous ribbon of concrete is a roof perched on seemingly randomly placed steel columns that wriggle across the site. On the plan the roof looks like a missing piece from a jigsaw puzzle, or an amoeba. Beneath the roof, recessed, full-height glass walls follow a different curved path held by green-painted walls to each end. The overall plan is a collision of curved forms – the flat but fluid roof, sinuous walls, muscular rock and egg-shaped pool – that are reminiscent of an abstract painting. To the south of the house is a straight line that turns out to be the edge of the site that drops to reveal bedrooms below. The house is approached from this side and entry is straight into the main space through a sliding glass screen. Once within, a curved screen reminiscent of Mies van der Rohe's Tugendhat House, clad in rich orange-coloured vertical timber boards, arrests the view and embraces a dining space. Turning slightly, the glass wall opens out onto the garden and the boulder crashes through the glass into the space. Behind the curved timber screen lies a cloakroom and a kitchen while a tapering staircase descends down the side of the boulder.

On the opposite side from the dining space, a living area is cocooned by an egg-shaped, full-height wall. Floors are in shiny brown tiles. The roof, white and pure with no light fittings, feels just like a cloud. Niemeyer described how he liked to watch clouds in the sky: 'Sometimes they are huge and mysterious cathedrals . . . other times, terrible warriors, Roman chariots riding through

NIEMEYER HOUSE (CASA DAS CANOAS), RIO DE JANEIRO, BRAZIL

the air, or unknown monsters running through the winds at full tilt, and more often, because I was always searching for them, beautiful and vaporous women reclining on the clouds, smiling at me from their infinite spaces.'

Between the side of the enormous boulder and one of the few straight walls in the house, painted with a verdant green gloss paint, the staircase slides down as if entering a grotto, landing in a central space with a parquet timber floor and a timber-lined storage wall to one side, and curved bookshelving to the other. This space receives modest daylight through a row of high-level circular clerestory windows. Arranged around this lie four bedrooms, three of which sit against the straight external wall that appeared below the entrance court. Each of these rooms has a central, truncated pyramidal window looking south into the forest that lends them a cave-like feel, in stark contrast to the open living spaces above.

Perhaps one of the most impressive qualities of the house is the way it responds directly to the site, achieving an integration with nature that recalls traditional Japanese architecture. The garden was designed by Niemeyer's friend Roberto Burle Marx, whom he had met as part of the team for the Ministry of Education building. Burle Marx was destined to become the leading landscape

141

architect in Brazil and pioneered the use of native tropical vegetation and free-form water features in the landscape.

Upon its completion on 1953, the house was quite unique in its fusion of modernist glass pavilion and curvilinear geometry. Mies's Farnsworth House, completed just two years earlier, offered a similar vision of living within a glass pavilion with internal walls seen as floating elements, subdividing space, but in a classical, rigid geometric form. Niemeyer sets this free in a playful, sensuous form, pushing the *plan libre* to new heights. The freedom was in the plan, for the horizontal planes remain rigidly straight. From the western end, looking at the kitchen prow, the house looks fairly mainstream and not dissimilar to Jan Duiker's Zonnestraal Sanitorium from 1931, with its curved glass windows sitting above a low rendered wall, beneath an overhanging flat roof.

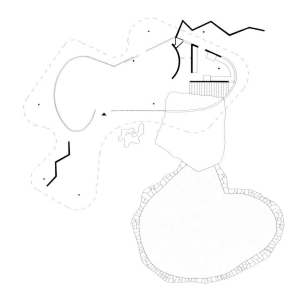

ABOVE:
JPA plan of Niemeyer House

OPPOSITE:
Interior view of Niemeyer House

The house drew much criticism in the early years from European architects, who were unconvinced by the stark contrast between the two floors, and its intensely personal, almost arbitrary qualities. But it was to influence a generation of architects as far afield as Australia, through the architecture of Harry Seidler, who had worked for Niemeyer for three months in 1948, and California, through the work of John Lautner. It remains a question whether Corbusier himself, seeing his young tyro's free use of the curve, was in turn encouraged to take his own playful forms further. Certainly, his work after 1950 shows this tendency, with the chapel at Ronchamp, completed in 1954, taking it to a poetic zenith.

As a member of the Brazilian Communist Party since 1945 and a close friend of Fidel Castro, Niemeyer and his family had to leave the house in 1964 when a right-wing military coup took control of the country. As a communist, his office was ransacked and publication of his work was suspended, and he was several times detained and interrogated by the military police. Forced into exile, he set up an office in Paris and worked on projects across Europe, Africa, Russia and the Middle East until the fall of the dictatorship and his return to Brazil in 1985.

After the Casa das Canoas, Niemeyer went on to build the new Capital complex in Brasilia. Among his lifetime output of over 600 buildings he was to complete 14 more houses, yet only three of these – the Simão, Mondadori and Ribeiró houses – continued his sinuous planning. His other houses played with angular geometries, with curved forms often set within the building, and in some cases he returned to traditional *fazenda* designs, using vernacular forms and materials.

In 2004, after 76 years of marriage, his beloved wife Annita died aged 93. Two years later, Niemeyer, at just short of his 99th birthday, married his long-term secretary, Vera Lucia Cabreira. Semi-retired at the age of 80, he famously continued to go to the office every day to work on projects for the rest of his long life until his death at 104. His daughter Anna Maria died the same year, so he left four grandchildren, 13 great-grandchildren and six great-great-grandchildren. The Casa das Canoas now belongs to the Niemeyer Foundation and is open to the public for visits.

MAISONS JAOUL, PARIS, FRANCE

Le Corbusier, 1955

WHEN FRANCE FELL UNDER Nazi control in June 1940, Corbusier and his wife Yvonne fled to the small town of Ozon in the Pyrenees and, while his partner and cousin Pierre Jeanneret became involved in the resistance, Corbusier felt his first duty was to architecture. He worked with the Vichy government under Marshal Philippe Pétain and formulated grand plans for what remained of France and its colonial empire, but he fell out of favour and so his services were terminated in July 1941. He returned to the Pyrenees, where he threw himself into painting and writing. While European immigrants such as Mies van der Rohe and Walter Gropius pursued the modernist agenda in America, Corbusier had little work until after the war, when, avoiding possible charges of collaboration, he gained the commission from the Minister of Reconstruction to establish prototypes for mass housing. This was to lead, after seven years, to the Unité d'Habitation in Marseilles that was completed in 1953. With material shortages the Unité was built in rough concrete, or *béton brut*, that contrasted well with the more limited use of steel and glass.

By the early 1950s, alongside larger commissions such as the pilgrimage chapel at Ronchamp (1955), the Monastery of La Tourette (1959) and the major buildings at Chandigarh (1955–8), Corbusier also spent four years working on a pair of houses in the suburb of Neuilly-sur-Seine. He was commissioned in 1951 to build the houses for an extended family – André Jaoul, a prominent industrialist, with his wife and younger son, and his older son Michel and his wife and three children. André Jaoul had met Corbusier on board the *Normandie* cruise ship heading for New York in October 1935 and they became friends. Theirs was something of a competitive friendship, both believing in pushing things forward in life – Jaoul one day boasted to Corbusier that he had given up smoking, saying, 'Very few people could do a thing like that after so many years', to which Corbusier responded, 'You think I can't?' 'I doubt it' said Jaoul. Corbusier had smoked pipes, cigars and cigarettes for decades and had a collection of 60 pipes. His jackets were tailored to incorporate purpose-made pockets for a box of 250 matches, which usually lasted only a day, but his pride made him give up that day. The two men also

BELOW:
Le Corbusier in *c.* 1957

shared a taste for contemporary paintings. Corbusier was to introduce André Jaoul to Jean Dubuffet and his circle, which eventually led to the collection of Dubuffet's paintings that ended up hanging on the walls of Jaoul's new house.

In 1937, Jaoul had asked Corbusier to design a weekend house in the style of a vernacular construction of rough timber logs, with a butterfly roof, floating over a free plan – a far cry from the Purist white houses of the 1920s. Having perfected his new Purist language, however, Corbusier, like his contemporary in the field of art, Picasso, moved on to a new means of expression. Perhaps the reality of weathering, with the pure white surfaces of his houses left out in the rain, cracking and staining, made him look for more durable materials. His belief in reinforced concrete – forged in his early years in the office of the pioneer Auguste Perret – was deeply held but now instead of being covered up it was to be expressed. His respect for and interest in craftsmanship (his father was after all a Swiss watchmaker, and he had apprenticed in this craft too) led him to look at vernacular buildings, where a marriage between place and materials was found.

In the decade between the Villa Savoye and the outbreak of the Second World War, Corbusier devoted his energies towards the bigger picture of cities and urban planning. He published his *La Ville Radieuse* (*The Radiant City*) in 1935, with its radical proposal to 'clean and purge' the European city, to create a classless sea of glass skyscrapers for the masses. He was a true polymath – architect, urban planner, painter, sculptor, writer – but, most of all, a polemicist. From the outset it was never enough for him to be a great architect, for he truly believed he could change the world. And he did.

Corbusier sketched out the prescient Maison Monol design in 1919, bringing vaulted concrete roofs to bear, a theme that reappeared with his design for a Maison d'Artiste in 1922. Sixteen years after the vaulted roof of his Monol design, the theme recurs for the Petite Maison de Weekend, built at Celle-Saint-Cloud in the western suburbs of Paris in 1935. This can be seen as a prototype for the Maisons Jaoul. Of course, the vault, in particular the traditional shallow Catalan vault, was not only evidence of the efficient use of brick but also seen in Perret's industrial thin concrete shells such as those used in the Casablanca docks – and, typically of a man with an eye on the future, in the arched roofs of railroad freight and Pullman cars.

He continued to develop projects using vaulted roofs across the 1940s with La Sainte-Baume hotel and housing in 1948 and the Roq et Rob hotel and housing designs for a site on the Côte d'Azur from the following year, which introduced

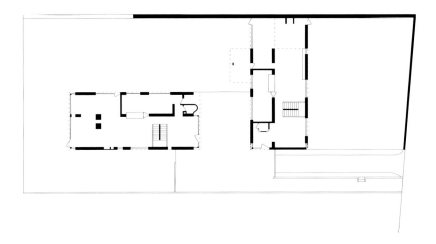

ABOVE:
Plan of
Maisons Jaoul

OPPOSITE:
Exterior view of
Maisons Jaoul

the idea of concrete vaulted roofs covered in grass. Then in 1950 he was asked by Professor Rudolph Fueter, a mathematician at Zurich University, to design a house on the edge of Lake Constance for his retirement. This design offers perhaps the most resolved of Corbusier's vaulted house designs – a modest single-storey house of rough brick, capped by a deep, five-bay undulating vaulted roof, covered in grass. Brick walls were also used internally and central to the composition was a fireplace. Before the house could be built, the Professor died, so Corbusier took the concept to the Jaoul project.

With the purchase of the plot on the Rue de Longchamp and believing Corbusier would be too busy with his large-scale projects such as the Unité building in Marseilles and the Indian projects in Chandigarh and Ahmedabad, the Jaouls contacted the English architect Clive Entwistle, something of a disciple of Corbusier who had initiated a collaboration with him on various projects back in the late 1930s, as well as translating his *Propos d'urbanisme* (*Concerning Town Planning*) in 1948. By June 1951 Entwistle submitted his design to Jaoul, only for him to ask Corbusier to examine the plans, which he did three weeks later. Corbusier was highly critical of his friend's decision to house both families in a single three-storey building and then visited the site three days later to announce that the Jaouls could have 'two houses for the price of one', walking away with the fib, and the job.

Having spent 32 years working on the idea of the vaulted structure and with the house for Professor Fueter abandoned after his death, Corbusier adopted the vaulted form straightaway. However, despite all the years of development,

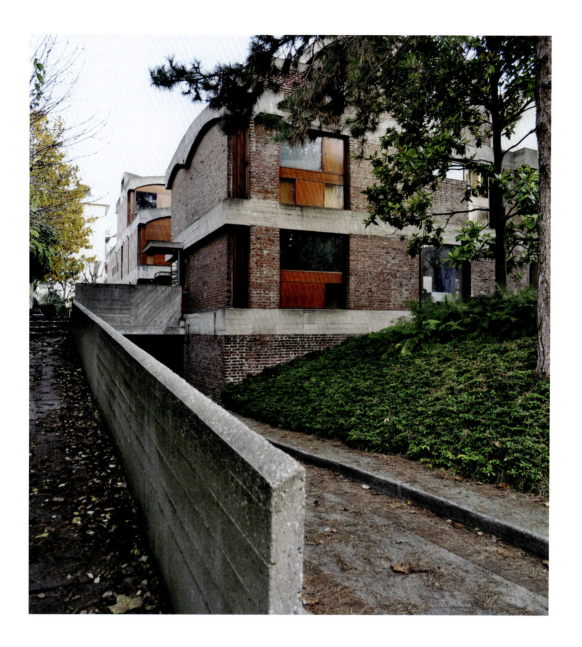

he struggled with the tightly constrained site from his first sketch design that July, with two parallel forms sitting side-by-side filling the site. This became two diagonally placed houses by November and a later plan stretched across to the neighbouring plot, before he arrived, in January 1952, at the final layout of two houses set at right angles to each other. It is reassuring that, even with his genius, it took him six months to arrive at the design (considerably longer than Frank Lloyd Wright's reputed two hours to dash off Fallingwater).

LEFT AND OPPOSITE:
Interior view of
Maisons Jaoul

The first house (usually referred to as House A) sits parallel to the road and straddles the site, save a ramp and driveway leading to an underground garage to one side. The second house (House B) sits behind the first and at right angles to it. The ramp arrives at a raised courtyard between the two houses and both entrances are arranged off this central space. Both houses employ the same basic plan of two asymmetric bays, the wider, at *c.*3.6 m (11 ft 9 in), providing the main living space at ground level, and the narrower, at *c.*2.25 m (7 ft 5 in), providing the kitchen and service spaces. The same layout orders the bedroom and bathroom spaces to first floor, while both have a smaller second-floor master bedroom suite.

From the street, the first house appears as a flat plane, two storeys high, with rough pink-red brick panels with thick, uneven mortar joints set between deep board-marked concrete bands. A smaller attic storey sits asymmetrically on top of this elevation. Windows read as deep apertures and the frames are in natural timber. At roof level, boxy concrete projections signal waterspouts, with downpipes buried in the brick piers below. The building looks industrial, with a strong leaning towards the primitive and vernacular. Michel Jaoul's daughter Marie, 29 years after moving into the second house, reflected that 'My school friends would say: "Why do you live in a factory? Don't your parents have any money?" They thought that it was a factory because it was not finished off like the others.'

The gable ends of the house, although blank, reveal at roof level the twin vaults, unified by an arched profile to the parapet and offering the enduring

image of the Jaoul houses. The upper house presents the gable as the front and has full-height timber screens set between the concrete bands, containing *pan de verre*, a kind of abstract timber composition of solid panels and glass, as if an excuse to demonstrate Corbusier's Modulor geometric system. The resultant brick, concrete and timber palette prefigures Louis Kahn's elemental designs of a decade later.

Within the houses, the roughness is tamed. While the terracotta tile vaults cover all ground floor rooms arching above cream tiled floors, elsewhere surfaces are generally plastered. In fact, the interiors are quite playful and colourful – gone are the pale shades of Purism in favour of bold primary colours, skewed to unique Corbusian hues that correspond to the palette he brought to his sculptures.

Both houses share the same organisation of side-by-side asymmetric vaulted bays, with a central wall that divides the larger spaces (living/dining/bedrooms) from the smaller supporting spaces (across the Atlantic, Kahn had codified his served and servant spatial planning approach a few years before). At ground floor both entrances greet the visitor with a sensually curved element containing a small bathroom. On the front house this leads directly into a hallway graced with a concrete zig-zag staircase, replete with a flat steel handrail that looks like an outline drawing for a Purist painting. On the rear house the hallway is to one side and the entrance leads more directly into the long, thin kitchen space. The living space of both houses occupies the whole width of the house at the furthest point from the entrance, with the central wall eroded and terminated as a fireplace. To the first floor, two bedrooms occupy the ends of each house with a third tucked in the middle, while bathrooms occupy the narrower bay. In the front house, occupied by André and Suzanne Jaoul, a small chapel was inserted by the main bedroom as a private place for prayer.

The families moved into their houses in October 1955, after André had died the previous November. They lived there happily for 32 years, but in 1987 both houses went to auction. They were bought by the British developer and collector of modern houses Lord (Peter) Palumbo, adding them to Mies van der Rohe's Farnsworth House in Illinois and Wright's Kentucky Knob in Pennsylvania. Palumbo looked after the houses well and made them very popular with architectural tourists and students but, after 12 years, sold them on to two sisters and their respective husbands in 2001.

During the period of the design and construction of the Maisons Jaoul, Corbusier was at last in demand again and at his artistic peak. His interest in the vernacular set him on course for a more primitive and sculptural language. The Villa Sarabhai in Ahmedabad, India, completed the same year as the Maisons Jaoul, was to be the last of the vaulted houses, and the most confident; this was a house with a series of tiled, vaulted, parallel bays oriented to catch the prevailing breeze, and projecting piers capped by concrete hoods create verandas or *brises-soleil*. Recently widowed, Manorama Sarabhai wanted a quiet place to live with her two sons and Corbusier generally stayed with the family on his trips to Ahmedabad throughout the 1950s. The house is like a stripped-back version of the Maisons Jaoul, a kind of polished primitive construction of vaults and concrete.

Ozon II, Sculpture 24, 1962

The Maisons Jaoul were to have a wide-ranging influence across Europe, while the Sarabhai house rippled across India in the works of Charles Correa and B.V. Doshi. The British architect James Stirling published an article in 1955 that was to launch a debate on the 'crisis of rationalism', proclaiming 'a philosophical change in attitude' and stating that, in the two houses, 'There is no reference to any aspect of the machine . . . either in construction or aesthetic'. Corbusier's change of direction immediately inspired Stirling, who went back to London and designed a low-cost group of houses on Ham Common near Richmond in Surrey (1958) that was closely based on the new, rugged aesthetic of brick and concrete, albeit with somewhat tidier brickwork.

Corbusier's fascination with *béton brut* (raw concrete) caught international attention with the Maisons Jaoul, and its influence went around the world for several decades under the banner of Brutalism. While it spawned some notable buildings by architects such as Basil Spence, Denys Lasdun, Stirling and the Smithsons in the United Kingdom, and Paul Rudolph in the United States, it became associated with failure as the concrete surfaces weathered badly in northern maritime climates and the social experiments in high-rise housing proved misguided.

If Corbusier's Villa Savoye is in some ways an architectural expression of his Purist paintings, then the Maisons Jaoul reflect his sculptures – muscular, crafted and hewn from natural materials.

STAHL HOUSE (CASE STUDY HOUSE 22), LOS ANGELES, CALIFORNIA, USA

Pierre Koenig, 1960

AN OPPORTUNE SNAP CAUGHT the moment when the photographer Julius Shulman perched precariously on a wall, about to take a photograph – one of many that saw him become the leading chronicler of what became known as Californian Modernism. The photograph he took in that instant captured the modest single-storey Stahl House, wrapped around a sky-blue pool and set upon the edge of a precipice. It encapsulated the American dream – blue skies, friends chatting by the pool, inviting sun-loungers, a wonderfully open living space, a car nestled under the roof and an expansive view across the city of Los Angeles. This was subsequently published in the *Arts & Architecture*

LEFT:
Julius Shulman photographing Stahl House, *c.*1960

OPPOSITE:
Pierre Koenig, *c.*1960

STAHL HOUSE (CASE STUDY HOUSE 22), LOS ANGELES, CALIFORNIA, USA

magazine in June 1960 and, like Bill Hedrich's photograph of Fallingwater some 15 years earlier, was destined to become one of the most iconic images of modern residential architecture.

Another of Shulman's photographs of the house that day has become something of a talisman for modernism, as Norman Foster summed up:

> I am thinking, of course, of the heroic night-time view of Pierre Koenig's Case Study House #22 which seems so memorably to capture the whole spirit of late 20th-century architecture. There, hovering almost weightlessly above the bright lights of Los Angeles spread out like a carpet below, is an elegant, light, economical and transparent enclosure whose apparent simplicity belies the rigorous process of investigation that made it possible. If I had to choose one snapshot, one architectural moment, of which I would like to have been the author, this is surely it.

The house is often referred to as Case Study House 22, as it was indeed the 22nd house in a series promoted and published by *Arts & Architecture* magazine, and it catapulted the 35-year-old Pierre Koenig firmly into the limelight.

With the completion of Case Study House 8 – the Eames House – in 1949, built entirely of prefabricated industrial components, *Arts & Architecture* spearheaded a new drive towards promoting steel frames and industrial materials.

From then on, architects such as Richard Neutra, Raphael Soriano, Craig Ellwood and then Koenig in 1958, with his first Case Study House 21 (Bailey House), championed the steel frame as the basis for the new ideal.

Pierre Francis Koenig was born to a mother of French and a father of German descent in San Francisco in 1925. Escaping the Great Depression, his family moved to the boom town of Los Angeles just as war broke out in Europe and where Koenig fell in with a group of friends who were set on studying architecture. He enlisted into the US Army's Advanced Special Training Programme in 1942, which promised an accelerated college education (four years into two) at the University of Utah, but found himself transferred into the

292nd Field Artillery Observation Battalion in Texas. Sent to the front lines in France and later Germany, he had to wait until 1946 to complete his studies, returning to the United States on the *Queen Mary*, which had been pressed into wartime service as a troop ship. After two further years of study at Pasadena City College he was determined to join the architecture course at the University of Southern California (USC). Places were hard to come by, but he waited every day from 8am until 5pm for a week outside of the Dean's office until he was finally admitted.

In his third year at USC, a tutor rejected his idea for a steel-framed housing project, declaring that 'steel was intended for industrial, rather than residential use', so he decided to prove him wrong. He gathered up his savings and took

ABOVE:
Exterior view of Pierre Koenig's Bailey House, Los Angeles, 1958

OPPOSITE:
Stahl House under construction, *c.*1959

out loans to build a small house for himself. After years on the front he clearly had little fear and was willing to take risks. He bought a small lot and set about building his first house while still a student. At only 93 sq m (1,000 sq ft), it was a one-bedroom house – a simple rectangle on plan, with a projecting carport at right angles. Beginning his lifetime collaboration with the engineer William Porush, the steel frame was set on a *c.* 3 m (10 ft) module, as this was the optimum span for the 38 mm (1½ in) steel decking. With corrugated steel siding and infill panels of plywood, the house has a very Japanese feel but, with exposed steel beams and decking internally, it was an elegant demonstration of industrially produced materials creating a convincing prototype for affordable housing when it was completed in 1950. It produced commissions as soon as he qualified and Koenig was able to perfect his initial experiment in industrial materials across the 1950s with five houses and a radio station building, but it is the 1959 Bailey House that *Arts & Architecture* hailed as 'some of the cleanest and most immaculate thinking in the development of the small contemporary house'.

Like Mies van der Rohe's Farnsworth House eight years previously, the Bailey House is a demonstration of distillation, of editing down the elements and the details to the minimum. Here, the vocabulary that Koenig had worked through

for nine years was refined and honed, resulting in only two steelwork details and a startlingly simple plan. Some 9 x 13.5 m (30 x 44 ft) in plan with solid ends and glazed on both of the long sides, the simple form was complemented by an open carport that projected forward to one side, creating an L shape. At the point where the carport meets the house, a square cut-out in the roof with a planter below creates a threshold to the house. Both house and its terraces are surrounded by a shallow pool that adds to the visual lightness of the building, accentuating the idea that it floats above the earth. It has the feeling of being a system – a kit of parts – and an exemplar model for mass production. It was also beguiling in its promise of the good life, again captured in the photographs of Shulman.

Buck Stahl, a retired professional football player, and his wife Carlotta bought a plot high up on the Hollywood Hills above Sunset Boulevard, paying just over the equivalent today of £100,000. Buck's family thought him crazy, but he had a clear idea of what he wanted and spent a couple of years hauling rocks up to the site at weekends, building retaining walls to stabilise the steep edges of the site for the future house. The Stahls spent several years interviewing architects, including Ellwood, before they saw one of Koenig's houses in a Sunday newspaper article and called him up. Buck Stahl was insistent, as Koenig recalled years later, that, 'I don't care how you do it, there's not going to be any walls in this wing. We did not want to lose any view anywhere.' This chimed perfectly with Koenig's work, and he was appointed in 1957. The clients wanted a spacious house with two bedrooms and a pool, but had what Koenig described as 'champagne tastes and a beer budget'.

The location was difficult – Koenig called it 'an eagle's nest' – but construction began in September 1959 and the house was built remarkably quickly, due to the steel frame and modular components. It was completed in May 1960 when it was opened up to the public as part of the Case Study Program. The furniture that was to appear in the Shulman photographs was loaned by Van Keppel-Green, but the Stahls had no money left to buy this, so it was returned after the public visits.

Koenig arrived at a simple L-shaped plan that turned its back to the street and created a courtyard facing the panorama. Anchoring the structure along the back of the site on an east–west axis with a concrete base, a second wing pushes out across to the edge of the hill on a series of reinforced concrete beams nearly 1 m (30 in) deep, supported by up to 10 m (35 ft) deep concrete pads. It cantilevers out 3 m (10 ft) above the street 40 m (125 ft) below.

Plan of Stahl House

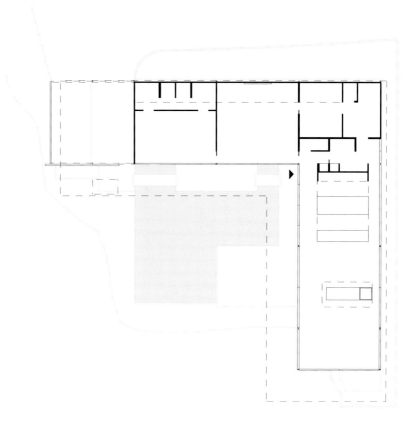

The steel frame, a simple welded construction of 30 cm (1 ft) deep 'I' beams and 10 cm (4 in) wide 'I' columns on a 6 m (20 ft) grid, defines the space. Exposed steel decking forms the roof plane. The elegance of this frame was given further expression by a 2.4 m (8 ft) overhang to the southern and western faces, providing solar shading and ample shelter to the poolside. By using deeper beams above square, narrow columns, the structure has a thrust towards the precipice that lends the building a dynamic and graceful quality.

The frame is enclosed by corrugated steel decking (as used on the roof but with a shallower profile), while the open sides are enclosed using 3 m (10 ft) wide sliding glass doors. The living wing, glazed on all three sides within the elegant frame, has great elan and offers a perfect demonstration of outdoor living, or at least living within a delicate shelter, able to engage with nature and the distant views.

At its heart, the living space has a small steel-framed fireplace structure that subtly subdivides the space without interrupting the roof plane that floats above – only a flue appears above the roof. The hearth is a constrained, raised rectangle of stone blocks – a kind of abstracted homage to Frank Lloyd Wright's boulder heaving up out of the floor at Fallingwater perhaps? The kitchen too is given its own frame, with a dropped ceiling enclosing a gridded lighting panel, fans and electrical supply. Along with the few stone blocks of the hearth, timber laminate on the kitchen cabinets offers the only natural materials in the house. The floors are in a smooth exposed concrete and were occasionally given some domestic relief by the use of rugs, while internal walls were plaster finished.

The bedroom wing provides two bedrooms enfilade – that is, one opening on to the next – so that the children had to cross their parents' bedroom to get to their own room; quite optimistic for parents with three children. The children's bedroom is then subdivided with a curtain and, behind the bedheads, separate washing areas are provided, with a shared central toilet and shower. The corner of the L-shaped plan provides the master bedroom with a large walk-through dressing room and bathroom. To the far end of the bedroom wing, the roof continues above an open carport and a gate then provides access to the courtyard – this is the entrance to the house. To get to the 'front door' – a sliding glass screen tucked in the corner of the living wing – involves a short journey beneath the roof overhang, across two raised concrete bridges or flat planes that cross the pool.

When the Stahls moved in, Buck installed wire fencing along the edge of the drop to catch his young children if they fell and later added a delicate timber walkway around the end of the living wing where it hung over the abyss to aid window cleaning, but apart from that the family lived in the house as built.

The house, of some 205 sq m (2200 sq ft), cost $34,000 to build (the equivalent of £218,000), with another $3650 (£23,000) spent on the pool, and it is rumoured that the Stahls were once offered $15 million (£12 million) for the house. After Buck Stahl died in 2005, the family sold the house at auction in 2007 for $3.1 million (£3 million).

The Eames House some 11 years previously had set the benchmark for the idea of creating homes using industrial materials, introducing steel framing and exposed steel decking as part of the domestic realm. Koenig had produced a stripped-back version of this with his Bailey House just the year before, but it was the Stahl House, with Shulman's brilliant photographs, that became the pin-up model for architecture in the 1960s. The house has featured in over 1200 newspaper and magazine articles, journals and books. It has also appeared in numerous films, television shows and commercials.

ABOVE:
Interior view of Stahl House

OPPOSITE:
Exterior view of Stahl House showing the pool and terrace.

STAHL HOUSE (CASE STUDY HOUSE 22), LOS ANGELES, CALIFORNIA, USA

Following the Stahl House, the Case Study Program continued but the experiment gradually lost sight of its original vision to provide models for affordable contemporary homes for the American family, with later houses attracting wealthy clients and creating larger and more opulent houses.

Koenig enjoyed his celebrity and work came his way, but in 1964 he decided to combine a modest practice with teaching, so joined USC as a professor. He continued his interest in low-cost production houses but failed to get federal funding to build his prototypes. He built nine more elegant houses that stayed with the kit of parts he had developed by 1960 but none were to match the Stahl House. He stayed at USC until his death from leukaemia in 2004, aged 78.

GWATHMEY HOUSE, AMAGANSETT, NEW YORK, USA

Charles Gwathmey, 1965

WHILE ALBERT EINSTEIN HAD PUBLISHED his general theory of relativity, Picasso had created Cubism, Seurat had painted his masterpiece *A Sunday Afternoon on the Island of La Grande Jatte* and Corbusier had built his Villa La Roche, all by the age of 27, architects rarely surface before the age of 40. It is often said that architecture is an old man's game, and Louis Kahn's overnight success at the age of nearly 50 is often quoted to prove the point, but there are exceptions, and the 27-year-old Charles Gwathmey's design for his artist parents, Robert and Rosalie, is certainly a case in point. Designed before he qualified as an architect, it immediately catapulted him into the limelight and, later, with the publication of the 1972 book *Five Architects*, to national prominence along with Richard Meier, John Hejduk, Michael Graves and Peter Eisenman.

At first sight, Gwathmey House appears as a piece of abstract sculpture. It appears to be made from board-marked concrete and it seems to be really quite big. In fact, it is none of these things, but a very small house built from timber. It is sited on a coastal strip on the east end of Long Island, in Amagansett, part of the now highly desirable Hamptons that have been home to many global stars such as Paul McCartney, Marilyn Monroe, Lou Reed and Scarlett Johansson. Built on a suburban plot some 400 m (1200 ft) back from the Atlantic Ocean, facing sand dunes and twisting slightly eastwards, with undeveloped land surrounding it (later built over), the house is only 111 sq m (1200 sq ft), yet given presence by a vertical emphasis.

During his studies, Gwathmey had toured Europe and had been captivated by the work of Corbusier and the chapel at Ronchamp in particular, with its sculptural force that had confirmed the idea of the architect as a form-maker, rather than a theorist. Gwathmey was to comment that, 'The objectiveness of Ronchamp was appealing. It clearly was a sculptural object that had presence by its existence on the site. I wondered how you could make a small building establish that same sense of place through its essence, undecorated, unadorned, relying on its form and its space and the idea of a single materiality.'

BELOW:
Charles Gwathmey in *c.*1980

OPPOSITE:
Exterior view of Gwathmey House

166

GWATHMEY HOUSE, AMAGANSETT, NEW YORK, USA

He originally wanted to build the house in concrete and cast it like a sculpture, but the budget of $35,000 provided a constraint that meant he reverted to a more traditional timber framework, clad inside and out in cedar boarding. To the passing motorist it surely is seen as a concrete building, so this sleight of hand means it has a warm, domestic feel that lends the house greater mystique. The house is very nearly a pure cubic form, but a second sleight of hand allowed the width to be increased a little to accommodate the internal programme and the form is then eroded, as if a solid mass has been sculpted out, to create a carport and balconies. To this subtractive composition, Gwathmey added a cylinder containing a staircase serving all three floors at the rear and a semicircular staircase to the front serving the terrace, while a triangular rooftop skylight served the top floor studio. Gwathmey described this composition of cubes, triangles and cylinders as 'a solid block that has been carved back to its essence'.

The ground floor has an open corner that serves as a carport and leads to the entrance door, with a small galley-style studio for Gwathmey's mother set beneath the curved staircase to the front and a couple of cupboard-like bedroom spaces for grandchildren as well as a bathroom off to one side. A spiral staircase that half protrudes out of the cubic form rises up and opens out into

LEFT:
Exterior view of Gwathmey House

OPPOSITE:
JPA plan of Gwathmey House

the Corbusian *piano nobile* with a dining space and a double-height living room to one side. A balcony is partially inset into the room and conceals a small kitchen to one side. The top floor is mostly empty space above the living room and terrace, but a bedroom to one side doubles-up as a studio beneath the dramatic triangular rooflight. If the rooms are all modest in plan, they appear very generous in reality as the section of the house exploits interlocking volumes around the double-height living space and this in turn fuses with the outdoor space of the balcony that is literally brought into the house.

Each elevation of the house is a demonstration of geometric clarity and balance, maintaining the abstract sense of the house as a work of sculpture. The front elevation is the most photographed and brings a Piet Mondrian painting

GWATHMEY HOUSE, AMAGANSETT, NEW YORK, USA

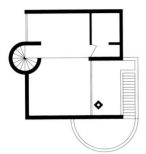

Third floor

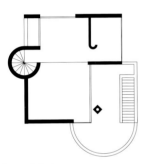

Second floor

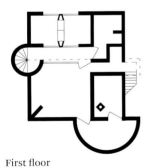

First floor

to mind, with solid and void balanced by a strip of red to one side, a yellow fascia bisecting the double-height glazing of the large inset balcony, and a white chimney, itself a square rotated at 45 degrees, that slices up through the void. The carved-out inset is balanced to one side by an almost blank wall, save a slot window halfway up lighting the kitchen. A small, solid-faced balcony projects forward off the bottom corner of the inset to signify the main entrance below, while the curved front staircase projects forwards and slides away from the inset. A more perfect elevational composition is hard to find.

The architectural language, while inspired and partly traceable back to early Corbusian houses, arrived fully formed. Perhaps the influence of one of his tutors, the architect Paul Rudolph, with his elegant series of houses built between the 1940s and 1950s, based on frames and incorporating inset courts and balconies, should be recognised. Equally, just as the world of art was centred on a few streets and squares in Florence in the 15th century, or a small quarter of Paris during the first decade of the 20th century, or the Bauhaus in the 1920s, where a large group of the most influential artists and architects were all teaching, so in New York in the 1960s, the New York Five were part of a small zeitgeist.

In 1969, an exhibition of photographs of five New York based architects was organised by the acronym-driven Committee of Architects for the Study of the Environment (CASE) at the Museum of Modern Art, and this spawned the book *Five Architects* that was to propel all concerned to international recognition. While not a 'group', they had all been mentored by Philip Johnson and were united by geography. Along with Gwathmey, then in partnership with Robert Siegel, a common allegiance to Corbusier's white houses in the 1920s and 1930s tied the architects together and so the group became known as the Whites or the New York Five.

Richard Meier had built many houses by the time the *Five Architects* book was published, but it was his first commission, for his parents Jerome and Carolyn, for a house in Essex Falls, New Jersey, that established his reputation. His subsequent Smith House of 1967 in Darien, Connecticut, looked across the Sound towards Long Island and was probably his finest house. A beautiful, white, abstract object that sits in, and alongside, nature as a clear creation of the intellect, it was also clad in timber, although stained white. It too

The living space of Gwathmey House

had a clear rectilinear form, here split between two basic forms that indicate private and public spaces, incised with inset balconies and supplemented by additive cylindrical staircases. His early houses established a fully resolved architectural language that has not varied across his long career, becoming arguably the most successful architect in America in the 20th century.

Peter Eisenman, Meier's second cousin, was perhaps the most original of the group. During the period between 1967 and 1978 he used single-family houses as a design vehicle to explore the essence of architecture. In ten numbered houses – four of which were built – he explored the transformation of what were essentially white cubes through a series of operations performed on an array of grids, planes and volumes, owing something of a debt to De Stijl. In the case of his seminal House X of 1975 for the Aronoff family, his early deconstructivist approach proved to be almost literal as it consumed his client's budget and then their savings in rectifying its faults. As an academic, his study on the Italian architect Giuseppe Terragni entitled 'From Object to Relationship', published in *Perspecta* magazine in 1971, was to rediscover the work of a master architect who had been ignored due to his association with the Italian Fascist Party under Mussolini.

John Hejduk's work lay between the fields of architecture, narrative, poetry and sculpture and was carried through drawings and writings rather than buildings, to generate a poetic version of the white buildings of his colleagues. His

GWATHMEY HOUSE, AMAGANSETT, NEW YORK, USA

House 10, illustrated in *Five Architects*, was a formal exercise of great beauty, balancing a series of geometric elements along an extended wall – it creates such poetry on paper that it is like a stanza from a Mozart concerto, or a painting by Paul Klee. Hejduk's work stands alongside Mies van der Rohe's design for a Country House as perhaps the most influential of the unbuilt projects of the 20th century.

Michael Graves was an architect who built a handful of highly experimental houses before he quickly shifted away from 'white' architecture towards the richness of postmodernism. His houses illustrated in *Five Architects* were more radical than those of Meier or Gwathmey, leaning towards the theoretical constructs of Eisenman and Hejduk. Within five years he had journeyed to what Vincent Scully described as 'the eternal battle with the keystone' with his first really postmodern building, the Plocek House. Perhaps his most successful design is a kettle, with a red whistle in the shape of a bird, for the Italian company Alessi in 1985, which remains the company's best-selling product.

Gwathmey was to go on, with Siegel, to build another dozen houses utilising the same architectural vocabulary and, in doing so, produced an enormously powerful and consistent body of work that perhaps lost some of its power as the scale and budgets increased, as the practice became the go-to architects for leading figures in the entertainment industry, such as David Geffen, Steven Spielberg and Jerry Seinfeld.

Gwathmey eventually inherited the house, by which time the Hamptons had become a fashionable weekender community and a large number of beach house imitations had sprung up around him. He was by then a very successful architect given to fast cars, Savile Row suits and John Lobb boots from London, and his practice with Siegel had grown into a large commercial enterprise producing buildings across all sectors, but the first dozen or so houses were never bettered.

Today, the house hides behind wire-mesh fencing and electric gates, screened from the road by tall hedging. The once rugged sea dune landscape is now manicured, with the hissing of summer lawns. Gwathmey died from oesophageal cancer in 2009 at the age of 71 but the practice survives as Gwathmey Seigel Kaufman Architects, with a portfolio of mainly large-scale civic projects, and very few houses. The Gwathmey House is no longer on the company's website.

FISHER HOUSE, HATBORO, PHILADELPHIA, USA

Louis Kahn, 1967

IN 1851, WITH THE CONSTRUCTION OF Joseph Paxton's Crystal Palace at the Great Exhibition in London, a new conception of space was born that was to change the course of architecture. It was the first large building to use the recently developed method for making cast plate-glass panels which were attached to a cast-iron framework to create what the German writer Lothar Bucher claimed was 'a revolution ... from which a new style will date' which, devoid of 'the play of shadows ... dissolved into a distant background where all materiality is blended into the atmosphere'. Exactly 100 years later, in 1951, with the completion of a small community bathhouse in Trenton, New Jersey, Louis Kahn single-handedly changed the course of architecture again, ending the dominance of the 'free plan' that had, since the early work of Corbusier, defined architecture in the first half of the 20th century.

The Trenton Bath House comprised four square pavilions with pyramidal roofs, linked around an open central court to assume a cruciform plan. Kahn's use of primary forms and geometries went back to ancient archetypes and his

LEFT:
Louis Kahn at his desk in *c.*1960

FISHER HOUSE, HATBORO, PHILADELPHIA, USA

RIGHT:
Louis Kahn's
Trenton Bath House,
New Jersey, 1951

BELOW:
Plan of Trenton
Bath House

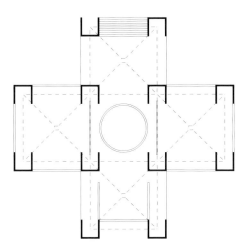

conception of space embraced the idea of discrete spaces – rooms – rather than the free plan which saw space as a continuous flowing experience. With the Trenton Bath House, Kahn famously declared that he found himself as an architect. Its architecture is formed by plain concrete block enclosing walls that recall Rome's Trajan's Market, capped by pyramidal roofs that float 30 cm (1 ft) above the walls and have an open oculus, again recalling a Roman precedent in the experience of the Pantheon. At once ancient and modern, the Trenton Bath House also crystallised Kahn's ideas on served and servant spaces, where a clear distinction is made in his designs between those spaces that serve, or support, primary spaces.

Louis Isadore Kahn, born Itze-Leib Schmuilowsky into a poor Estonian Jewish family, arrived in America as a five-year-old in 1906. His parents were seeking a new life and his father was avoiding conscription into the Russo-Japanese war. Louis's face and hands had been severely burnt in an accident when he was three and he was to carry this disfigurement all his life. Perhaps due to this early misfortune, his mother nurtured his talent in music – she was a talented musician herself (family tradition held that she was related to the German Romantic

175

composer Felix Mendelsohn), while his father's abilities in stained-glass craftsmanship saw him encourage Louis's skills at drawing. The Kahns (the family changed their name in 1915) settled in the Northern Liberties, a poor immigrant district to the north of Philadelphia. Excelling at school, Kahn was set to study painting at the Pennsylvania Academy of Fine Arts, but after taking a course in architectural history taught by William F. Gray he was smitten and joined the University of Philadelphia's School of Architecture instead. There he was taught under the Beaux-Arts teaching system, which was founded on a belief in the primacy of classicism. In 1928, he travelled across Europe for almost a year, spending five months in Italy where the ruins of ancient Rome were imprinted on his mind. In the early 1930s, Kahn spent years unemployed through the recession until he gained work in various offices mainly working on large-scale housing projects. He set up his own practice in the autumn of 1947 at the age of 46, mainly on a series of one-off house commissions which he combined with two days a week teaching at Yale University. The experience of teaching allowed Kahn to explore new concepts and, in particular, that of existentialist philosophy, with its emphasis on questions of being and becoming that were to inform his own highly philosophical approach to architecture.

Returning to Rome on a three-month post as the architect in residence at the American Academy in late 1950, Kahn studied the city's monumental buildings, stripped of their decoration to ruins, revealing brick arches, concrete structures and vaults. On his return to the United States, he never again used lightweight steel structures as he had done for his last commission before his trip, building only with concrete and masonry.

Dr Norman and Doris Fisher had bought a 6000 sq m (1.5-acre) plot bisected by the Pennypack Creek in Hatboro, a northern suburb of Philadelphia, in 1957. Keen to build a modern house they resorted to a telephone directory to find an architect and, intrigued by a reference to Kahn while interviewing a firm of architects, sought him out. Picking him up from the station to visit the site, Dr Fisher wrote of their first encounter that,

> On first contact Mr. Kahn did not make an impressive appearance. He was short in stature and had a badly burned face from a childhood accident. He wore black jackets, frequently shiny from wear. These superficialities soon faded, as his intellect, energy, humor and warmth showed through. He worked intensely with his yellow paper and black charcoal and in short time, a room or home appeared, peopled and landscaped.

FISHER HOUSE, HATBORO, PHILADELPHIA, USA

TOP:
View of Fisher House from across the Pennypack Creek

BOTTOM:
Exterior view from outside the entrance to Fisher House

Kahn was clearly a man of great charisma and many of his clients testified to his charm and warmth (it is hard not to be moved by the poignant interviews with his friends and patrons in his son Nathaniel's 2005 film *My Architect*). This was to be just as well, as it took nearly seven years before the family were able to move into their new house in June 1967, leaving the nine months it took Frank Lloyd Wright to design Fallingwater somewhat in the shade. After four different designs, one of which was to be costed at five times over budget, he finally came up with the design of two intersecting cubic volumes, which he characterised as 'a wood house on a stone plinth', in January 1964.

The Fisher House is quintessentially Kahnian, containing served and servant forms in a bold geometric composition. There are two cubic volumes, one containing bedrooms tilting away from the street but aligned north–south, the other set at 45 degrees to it, so that its principal facade looks north-east onto the creek below. The served space, containing a double-height living area, is skewered at one corner by the servant bedroom volume, connected with a 1.2 m (4 ft) high opening – a kiss between the two parts of the house.

Kahn was to complain that he just could not design houses and it is true that he was an architect that excelled at scale, as the monumental came naturally to him. Many of his greatest buildings over the years were a development of the design for the Fishers, including the Indian Institute of Management in Ahmedabad (1974) and the sublime National Assembly Building of Bangladesh in Dhaka (1982). The same compositional approach was evident in his unbuilt project for a Dominican Motherhouse (1965–9) where he arranged geometrically pure elements that are almost collaged together, with forms rotated to connect at corners in the way that the Fisher House's two forms collide. Scaling this down to a small house may have taken time but it produced one of the most original and abstract houses of the 20th century.

It is the abstraction of the house that is the primary impression that greets the visitor – it does not look like a house, especially set among its provincial neighbours, but appears instead as two enigmatic wooden boxes, large enough

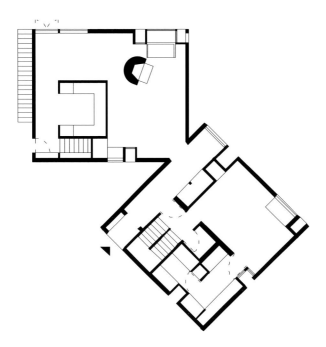

to be two-storey, with incised slits rather than window openings and no visible front door. A smaller timber-clad box containing garden equipment frames an access path directing visitors to the entrance along one side. Finally arriving at the deeply recessed front door, a second wooden box is apparent, set at a 45-degree angle to the front volume. A flight of steps runs along its side, dropping down the slope a full storey, revealing a base of Montgomeryville stone, a local reddish-brown sandstone common to the locality, which is carved out to provide storage space.

From the garden side, the house does indeed appear as a wooden house on a stone plinth, just as Kahn had described it. The narrow cypress vertical boards bisected by a horizontal trim at window head height are capped at the roof by a lead-coated copper trim that he also used on the windowsills. Although Kahn imagined the timber would naturally weather to a silver patina, the Fishers painstakingly applied a protective coloured stain that lends a yellowish hue, which happily reinforces the sense of the timber boxes as if they were pieces of fine furniture. This sense of cabinetry is further enhanced by Kahn's approach to fenestration, where he cuts out large geometric apertures – slots or squares

ABOVE:
Plan of Fisher House

OPPOSITE, TOP:
Interior view showing the fireplace of Fisher House

OPPOSITE, BOTTOM:
Norman and Doris Fisher in the living room of Fisher House, c.1958

FISHER HOUSE, HATBORO, PHILADELPHIA, USA

– and then partially infills them again with crafted timber elements to create opening panels for ventilation. The windows are largely simple fixed panes, set close to the face of the cladding.

Internally, the house has very narrow red oak floorboards that follow the geometry of each cube – interestingly, for an architect who dealt with Platonic forms, he allowed the practicalities to slightly deviate from the pure geometry, so each cube is a slightly different dimension, with the living cube allowed to be some 1.5 m (5 ft) off square in plan – and the walls are finished in a slightly sandy grained plaster that allows light to create, in Khan's words, 'a beautiful patina' on vertical surfaces. Plain oak skirtings and frames around openings combine with an oak staircase to set a very natural palette that is enhanced further by a Montgomeryville stone fireplace. This fireplace is part of one of Kahn's most recognisable set pieces, with fireplace, window and window seat combining into a beautiful domestic composition. The fireplace is set at 45 degrees (so aligning with the adjoining bedroom volume) to the double-height living room and has a curved back to the dining space. The double-height window is split by a transom at storey height, so that a giant pane of glass occupies the top, while below, Kahn creates a wonderful piece of joinery that incorporates inset bays to each side of a floating window seat. The bays have both fixed glazed panels and timber opening panels, to give control over light and air while also providing a deep recess to cradle the seat within a deep windowsill above. The fireplace almost touches the inset bay, so provides a tension that ensures this corner of the living space is the centrepiece of the house. Diagonally opposite this corner is a kitchen, set within a storey-height plastered box within the

FISHER HOUSE, HATBORO, PHILADELPHIA, USA

volume. The 'service' cube has two floors, with the entrance at ground and a bedroom and bathroom on each floor.

Once completed, the house did not cause much interest in architectural circles and it was perhaps seen as something of an oddity. It did not really look like a house, it had a plan like nothing seen before in domestic architecture and was modest in size. His Korman House, completed six years later in 1973, did find critical acclaim, and it is true that it masterfully codifies Kahn's approach to domestic design. While the Korman House is again based on his served and servant philosophy, and more recognisable as a house, I feel that it lacks the raw power and clarity of the two colliding cubes of the Fisher House.

For a short, disfigured man with a strange voice (scarlet fever as a child had raised its pitch), Kahn was indeed an enigma. For an architect who compartmentalised his buildings, it was perhaps less surprising to learn, after his death, of his multiple lives. Although he was married to his wife Esther from 1930 until his death and had a daughter, he also had two other families: one with his assistant Anne Tyng, who had daughter in 1945; and, later, with Harriet Pattison, with whom he had a son.

The living room window of Fisher House

SAN CRISTÓBAL, MEXICO CITY, MEXICO

Luis Barragán, 1968

COMMISSIONED BY THE SWEDISH businessman Folke Egerstrom and built between 1966 and 1968 in a northern suburb of Mexico City, Cuadra San Cristóbal is a private house with a stable and horse pool. Upon completion its architect, Luis Barragán, was relatively unknown outside of Mexico. He was to be 74 before his accomplishments were finally recognised with a retrospective of his work at the Museum of Modern Art in New York in 1976. He went from obscurity to celebrity overnight.

Luis Ramíro Barragán Morfín was born in 1902 in Guadalajara, in the state of Jalisco, the third of nine children. His parents were wealthy Mexican aristocrats who owned several ranches, so he grew up to be a good horseman and a devout Catholic. He graduated as a hydraulic engineer in 1923 but, with a strong interest in architecture, his family paid for him to spend two years travelling in Europe where, of course, he fell under the spell of Corbusier's new creations. Visiting the Alhambra, with its sequence of fountains and garden spaces – and having an admiration for the French painter and landscape architect Ferdinand Bac – Barragán was struck by the mystical power

LEFT:
Exterior view of
San Cristóbal

184

SAN CRISTÓBAL, MEXICO CITY, MEXICO

Luis Barragán, 1963

of gardens. By the time he returned home, he saw himself as a landscape architect.

The early years of his career in Guadalajara were unremarkable, and his work was founded on his fascination with Islamic architecture, particularly that from Morocco, fused with other Mediterranean influences. Moving to Mexico City in 1936, his work immediately became more influenced by the International Style, as he created cubic, abstract forms. It was, however, to be his own house, completed in 1947, that showed he was indeed an architect, and a consummate one at that.

Occupying two adjacent lots, numbers 12 and 14, on General Francisco Ramírez Street in a working-class neighbourhood of Mexico City, Barragán's own house appears unremarkable, austere even, in a rough-painted cement render and with only a square, projecting bay at the first floor hinting at a domestic life within. Number 12 was his studio, while 14, at roughly twice the size, was his home. Introspective and humble, the guarded house protected the private life of the architect.

Once within, rooms appear to dissolve one into another with single and double-height spaces interlocking, and walls not always taken up to the ceilings – these are formed of the exposed beams of traditional construction, creating detached horizontal planes. A graceful staircase in pine boards cantilevers out from the wall and rises up to a door that is enigmatically always closed. Materials are left in their natural state with rough plastered walls, volcanic rock tiles, polished wood floors side by side with rich Mexican ceramics. The house speaks of the vernacular architecture of ranches, villages and convents, while being infused with a hint of the spatial complexity of Adolf Loos – and even the planar abstractions of De Stijl.

Here, Barragán developed his interest in fusing indoor spaces with gardens and courtyards. The largest window, its glass divided into four panes by mullions that depict a cruciform, opens into the garden at ground level. The roof, however, becomes an abstract garden, a series of tall courtyard spaces. One court has a large relief crucifix set against the wall, while others are more abstract

TWENTY GREAT HOUSES OF THE TWENTIETH CENTURY

echoing Giorgio de Chirico, with an enigmatic emptiness, yet also fused with the poetic power of the pink and red hues of the enclosing walls. This metaphysical roofscape is surely one of the most remarkable labyrinths in the world, reminiscent of the writings of his Argentinian contemporary Jorge Luis Borges. While it brings Corbusier's Villa Savoye to mind, this rooftop has no interest in sun worship, although that may have been apt in the land of the Aztecs, but rather evokes the surreal world of Antoni Gaudí's Casa Milà from 1912. It opens up only to the sky – indeed Barragán raised the walls higher in 1954 to keep out any view of Mexico City's growing skyline.

Barragán successfully threw a wall around his private life too – 'My house is my refuge' he wrote, 'an emotional piece of architecture, not a cold piece of convenience'. This was a very poetic challenge to Corbusier's 'machine for living in'. 'The Mexican searches for the silence of closed worlds', wrote the Nobel Prize-winning novelist Octavio Paz, and so Barragán kept his life private, always living alone in a monastic existence, as his own house, full of single beds and Madonnas on the walls, confirms. He was tall, bald from puberty, blue-eyed and liked to wear English sports jackets, silk shirts and knitted ties. He enjoyed reading Proust and listening to classical music. In a different culture, he would have been called a dandy. He had a Cadillac and employed a chauffeur. He enjoyed melon halves drizzled with sherry and was known to have his maid prepare entirely pink meals. On Sundays he spent his time at an equestrian club and when someone accused him of 'only designing homes for rich people', he allegedly replied, 'And horses'. Perhaps not surprisingly, rumours at the time suggested that he was homosexual. What is certain is that he was under the heel of the Catholic faith, with all its contradictions.

In the early 1940s, Barragán announced to his friends his early retirement, apparently weary from the demands of private clients, and began purchasing land to develop for himself. He bought and developed several sites on the outskirts (now within the suburbs) of Mexico City in the following two decades, creating masterplans for residential districts that had landscaped spaces at their heart.

In 1958, foregoing early retirement, he began work on a residential project about 20 km (12 miles) north-west of the city known as Las Arboledas. He planned the infrastructure around his passion for horses so, at its centre, he created a public space where he abstracted nature with a series of walls, fountains and drinking troughs. This extraordinary space, a kind of plaza, had three main elements set around a processional avenue of eucalyptus trees. The first is a long red stucco wall ('the Muro Rojo') over 100 m (320 ft) long that disappeared

Interior view showing the living room of Barragán's house

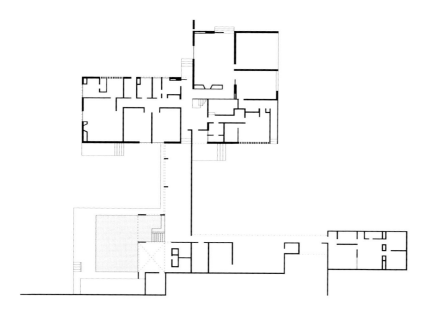

over the horizon. Conceived as the entrance to the French Riding School that established itself there, the wall has a sculptural and mysterious quality. The second, set to one end of this linear landscape, is the Plaza del Campanario (Plaza of the Bell). Here a pool is enclosed by ochre red walls, and a spout to one corner allows water to gush into a geometric reflecting pool so that the sound of water provides a constant background. The pools are enclosed by a palisade of tree trunks and a stand of eucalyptus. The third, at the opposite end of the ensemble, is the Plaza y Fuente del Bebedero (Plaza and Fountain of the Trough). This is a resting place where horses can be watered and is organised by a long, raised water trough in black stone. Full to the brim, with hidden water outlets and edged with a narrow drip gutter, the trough creates a mirror-like surface that reflects the trees and sky. This Alhambra-like trough is terminated by a tall white monolith, some 15 m (50 ft) high by 10 m (32 ft) wide, so that it closes the perspective and provides a blank canvas for nature's shifting shadows. This geometric composition of a long, low element and a tall vertical plane that never touch recalls the art of De Stijl and Mies van der Rohe's Country House project, fused with the surreal stillness of René Magritte or de Chirico. It is quite unique.

Barragán ennobled the wall at a time when architects around the world were dissolving the wall in favour of glass skins. He took the oldest architectural

ABOVE:
Plan of
San Cristóbal

OPPOSITE:
Exterior view
showing the
horse pool at
San Cristóbal

SAN CRISTÓBAL, MEXICO CITY, MEXICO

element and invested it with dignity and gravitas. It was to be the foundation of his architecture – earthbound, autonomous, protective – providing shade and shelter with a human scale and meaning. And then he began to paint the walls in vivid colours: terracotta and rusty reds, fuchsia pinks and purples, golds and aquamarine blues – all somehow intrinsically Mexican, yet also as avant-garde as the cut-outs that the bed-bound Henri Matisse was making at the same time.

In 1961 Barragán extended the Las Arboledas development with the acquisition of the adjacent site across a small stream. This was to be Los Clubes, a smaller residential quarter that was also to be based on equestrian principles. It is entered through an enormous wooden gateway, reminiscent of an old hacienda, that is framed by a wall to one side and a cubic volume to the other that served as a porter's lodge, both painted a bright pink. The estate was planned with large plots for detached mansions and again Barragán placed a fountain at the centre. The Fuente de los Amantes (Lover's Fountain) is a place where

horses can water. It occupies a corner lot, some 30 m (100 ft) wide by 42 m (138 ft) long. Two tall stucco walls in bright pink form a corner but again do not touch, framing the small plaza. Within, two rust-coloured stucco walls are set at right angles to each other and connected by a girder – an aqueduct – that carries water, gushing out at one end into a shallow pool below. The ground, paved with cobblestones, gently slopes into the water to allow horses to wade in. At the pool's edge two old wooden troughs were placed up-ended, whose sculptural representation of a couple leaning against each other lent the fountain its name, although these were sadly lost many years ago.

Within Los Clubes, Barragán was to build his masterpiece for a friend from the equestrian club he frequented. It had to be his dream commission – a family home with stables as the Egerstrom family bred and trained racehorses. San Cristóbal was built on a 3 hectare (7.5 acre) plot, and there are some 2500 sq m (2700 sq ft) of buildings, covering less than 10 per cent of the plot. It is a family house, but one that extends out to stable horses, creating an indivisible ensemble.

The plot is split roughly into four equal quadrants; a field, paddock, stables and stamping ground that occupy the top two quadrants to the north, a field in the south-east corner, and the house to the south-west corner. The site is entered through a covered gate that forms part of guest (once staff) quarters to the east, and a carport and service spaces to the west. Arriving into the paved entrance court, a covered walkway leads to a gate that pierces a long white stucco wall which opens into the domestic realm. The house sits either side of the wall, with a small inset doorway set against the wall facing the entrance court. The building presents a white cubic volume, containing the service rooms with a single long window shielded by slats that opens into the kitchen. To the corner, the end wall peels away to become a freestanding plane, sandwiched around a few steps that lead to a back doorway.

A partially covered swimming pool lies directly within the gate, surrounded by a lush garden. A wide covered walkway, with exposed roof beams behind the blank wall, leads directly to the front door. Once within, a tall hallway contains a staircase. The white wall carries on through the house and a sliding door opens into a back garden where the wall transforms into a fuchsia pink. To the left of the entrance are three large bedrooms and bathrooms, to the right beyond the staircase lies a large living room that projects back from the rectangular form of the main body of the house. The living room becomes L-shaped once a large sliding screen that separates it from a dining space is opened. The rooms are white, no exposed beams, just linked cubic volumes and wooden floors. A large window to the end of the living room slides away into the wall, opening up into the stable courtyard. A single door leads out from the living room into a walled courtyard, open only to the east.

The wall that runs through the house then continues on its north–south axis for another 75 m (250 ft). This pink wall, some 5 m (15 ft) tall, divides the stable courtyards from a field, linked by twin openings. To the east, 35 m (115 ft) away, a long stable building encloses the courtyard paddock that is given a north–south emphasis by a pair of long, low timber hitching rails. The stable is fronted by a timber-framed loggia sitting beneath a sloping roof covered in clay tiles. The southern wall of the stable block is a twin wall in a red coloured stucco that channels water, gushing out into a large shallow horse pool at the epicentre of the whole composition. It splits the stables from the entrance court and the domestic realm. Enclosing the northernmost end of the courtyard is another tall, pink wall, incised by two vertical slots that evoke defensive structures, which conceals the haystacks beyond. The colour palette is completed at the end of this wall with a lower, purple painted wall and matching metal-faced gate that closes the composition.

At San Cristóbal, Barragán's philosophy of seeing the garden as the primary living space and the house itself as an adjacent area of retreat is evident in one of the most startling, abstract and poetic works of the 20th century. It bears testimony to the great Mexican novelist Carlos Fuentes's words that 'There is no creation without tradition; the "new" is an inflection on a preceding form; novelty is always a variation on the past'.

Barragán was to suffer a long demise with Parkinson's disease that began shortly after his final 'equestrian trilogy', and he was feted in his mid-seventies with the 1976 retrospective of his work in New York. He was awarded the Pritzker Prize, the highest award in architecture, in 1980, and he died in 1988 at the age of 86. His ashes were interred at the Rotonda de los Jaliscienses Ilustres in Guadalajara, where the most celebrated citizens of the state of Jalisco are entombed. His own house and studio were declared a UNESCO World Heritage Site in 2004. In September 2015, the American conceptual artist Jill Magid gained consent from the family to take some of Barragán's ashes and use them to create a diamond. The following April, 2.02 carats' worth, rough-cut, with one polished facet arrived at her home in Manhattan, where it remains. It is a somewhat bitter irony that a man of soul and colour ended up as a hard, colourless gem.

CAN LIS, PORTO PETRO, MAJORCA

Jørn Utzon, 1972

FOLLOWING HIS VICTORY IN THE 20TH-CENTURY'S biggest architectural competition for the Sydney Opera House in 1957, nothing was ever going to be the same again for Jørn Utzon and his family. Working from Denmark for a number of years, they finally moved out to Sydney in 1962 and, as a family who had always loved the sea and beach life, found themselves in heaven. Anticipating their move to Australia as permanent, the Utzons bought 2.4 hectares (6 acres) of what at that time was inexpensive seafront land in the Sydney suburb of Bayview Heights. Utzon battled with the planners for nearly two years and produced four schemes before finally achieving consent only months before the Opera House saga reached its tragic climax as a new Government used Utzon as a scapegoat for cost overruns on the previous regime's flagship project and he and his family were forced to leave Sydney and his unfinished Opera House, never to return. The Bayview site proved to be not only an unfulfilled dream but, in exile, a shrewd if bittersweet investment that sold for a small fortune, the proceeds of which were sufficient to purchase two sites in Majorca.

Jørn and Lis Utzon first visited Majorca in 1957 on a sojourn from their work in Sydney to visit Lis's mother and Jørn had designed a small holiday village there for children who had suffered in the post-war polio epidemic. Although the design remained as a series of pencil drawings, the plan, like Frank Lloyd Wright's Fallingwater, was built around a series of giant rocks and this almost anticipated his later fascination with the stone and rugged terrain of Majorca.

BELOW:
Jørn Utzon, c.1960

OPPOSITE:
Can Lis viewed from the sea

Visiting again in the late 1960s after their exile from Australia, the Utzons found a landscape and climate that echoed that of New South Wales. While visiting friends in the Migjorn area in the south-east corner of the island, they made a trip out into the countryside and Lis, with her command of several languages, approached a group of three farmers and asked if there was any land for sale. One farmer spoke English and told of three sites: 'Beautiful, Marvellous and Paradise'.

They promptly bought both 'Marvellous' and 'Paradise', the first perched on a clifftop just outside the village of Porto Petro, the second on the hills about 10 km (6 miles) inland near the village of S'Horta on the slopes of the mountain beneath an ancient Moorish fort.

It was to be the site on the clifftop that was chosen as their home – the Utzons had always lived by the sea – and the first plans were sketched out in 1970. The house was named Can Lis in honour of Utzon's wife and they lived there in quiet seclusion for nearly a quarter of a century. They only moved when the glare from the sea became too much for the architect's sensitive eyes after years of working under an anglepoise lamp (Utzon was rarely seen without a jet-black pair of Raybans to protect his eyes). The rigours of moving from room to room in the outside weather also became more demanding with the passing of the years, especially through the cool winter months. Majorca's addiction to tourism must have had some part in their decision to eventually leave the house and move up the mountain to 'Paradise', as a Club 18–30 holiday camp was developed within earshot and their increasing infamy began to bring tourist coaches, intrepid architecture students and passing glass-bottomed boats whose tour guides would pronounce loudly across the sea that: 'THIS IS THE HOUSE OF THE ARCHITECT WHO DESIGNED THE SYDNEY OPERA HOUSE'.

The Bayview house designs in Sydney were where the language of the Majorcan houses was worked out – an architectural vocabulary of courts and linked elements that began with his first house in Hellebæk. This had begun the theme of a house sheltering behind a wall, yet it was his fascination with the courtyard houses of ancient China and north Africa that provided the real inspiration for this otherworldliness of the house behind, or within, a wall. Utzon visited the site on the clifftop before the house was built and climbed down the ledges of the cliff to sit in a cave almost directly below and enjoy the absolute unity of place and view, of shelter and exposure, and this became the feeling he wanted to recreate in his new home.

The first plan for the houses is dated November 1970 and it is named as 'Casa Olicia'. It takes the theme of the Bayview designs but distributes three blocks along a linear court nestling behind an unbroken wall, save the entrance off Calle de la Media Luna (Half-Moon Street). The key elements are already in place in embryonic form – the defensive wall, the colonnaded, stoa-like court opening out to the sea, the angled living room replete with funnel-shaped window bays, and cave-like bedrooms with cradled bed spaces and further projecting bays. Perhaps the most striking aspect of this design is the openness of the composition, with the whole plan spread-eagled around the single entrance court like two hands spread towards the African coast beyond the horizon.

The final plan was initially modelled by Utzon in sugar cubes, and then drawn for the authorities by his son Jan and adjusted, fine-tuned and created by the masons and Utzon himself *in situ*. The house has the appearance of a beautifully crafted work of geometry, something classical that fell from the skies and crashed onto the stone platform of the clifftop to adjust itself to the nature of the place. Utzon liked to say, with extraordinary understatement, that it was all so simple, 'no more than the way birds know instinctively where to nest on a cliff-top'. The house, almost a small village in stone, seems as if it has been there for centuries, yet it also feels so unique and new.

TOP:
View from the cave below Can Lis, which provided inspiration for the house

BOTTOM:
View along the clifftop towards Can Lis

TOP:
Exterior view of Can Lis from the cliff edge

BOTTOM:
Plan of Can Lis

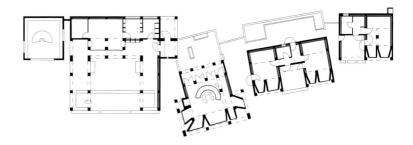

Arriving on a scruffy road with houses dotted along one side among thick scrub, there is no hint of the sea –or that a cliff edge is only some 20 m (65 ft) away. It is easy to pass Can Lis unnoticed, for its street facade is less than low-key – little more than a series of walls. Only the glazed tiled bench sitting beneath a rudimentary porch, with its blank, grainy wooden door, hints at a domestic world beyond. A crescent-shaped incision in the wall offers the first tantalising glimpse of the ocean beyond. This moment is twinned with a realisation that two open spaces await either side. The crescent, framed in dark blue and white glazed geometric tiles, points left but the overwhelming pull is right, into a nine-square courtyard framed by stoa-like colonnades that open out to the sea.

The courtyard is surprisingly small, intimate even, but this quality is immediately juxtaposed by the vastness of the sea, the sky and their meeting at the horizon. This courtyard is the anchor to the house – a house that reveals itself to be a chain of five blocks – and sits square to the cliff-face some 30 degrees east of due south. It immediately brings to mind ancient Greece with its colonnades and stoas and this is fused with the generosity and heroic nature of opening onto the sea, something that echoes in miniature Louis Kahn's Salk Institute court in California, which faces the Pacific, half a world away. This courtyard leaves no doubt that the house is dedicated to nature – to the path of the sun across the sky above the sea.

LEFT:
Exterior view of the entrance to Can Lis

OPPOSITE:
The courtyard of Can Lis

To the rear of the court lies the fairly rudimentary kitchen occupying two square bays divided into pantry and cooking areas with all the kitchen furniture built in thin stone slabs with white tiled surfaces. Shuttered windows open out onto the street beyond. A further two bays form a dining space with a built-in pine bench around a large table and two large window bays that project out beneath the colonnade roof; a final bay forms a small store. Each space is modest and possesses a raw domestic quality – no formica, stainless steel or kitchen gadgets here – that gives a sense of outdoor living, and an earthy natural life. The only hint of sophistication is the aluminium light fitting running across the back wall of the dining space, but yet again this is brought down to earth by the bare light bulbs plugged in like rivets.

Utzon's lifelong interest in the way nature constructs itself and his development of an 'additive architecture' is the basis for the construction of the house. The kit of parts – stone blocks, concrete 'I' beams and curved tiles – provides not just a dimensional logic, but a constructional DNA that grows the building into a unified whole. Horizontal structure is founded on standard precast concrete 'I' beams that can span up to about 5 m (16 ft 4 in), and these are used singly as supports for roof structures and doubled up as lintels for wall supports. Utzon recalled how he noticed the arched clay tiles in a local baker's shop one morning and knew that was what the roofs at Can Lis, then under construction, had to be. These *bovedillas*, once common in the region, had in fact ceased to be produced some years earlier, but Utzon's master builder knew where these were once made so they returned to the works, found the original

wooden curved moulds and set about making them. The tiles are made from flat clay slabs that are placed wet onto the mould where they quickly slump and assume the curved profile; these are then slid off to rest on their edges and dry in the sun. In this way, Utzon rediscovered and revived a small fragment of Majorcan vernacular: the tiles are still in manufacture today. Each *bovedilla* is placed between the flanges of the spanning 'I' beam, covered with flat clay tiles and finished in waterproof quarry tiles. These mini-vaults are appropriate to an architect who so frequently saw the roof as a cloud floating above space – from the rolling trade-wind clouds of his Bagsværd Church to the epic vaults of the Opera House – and the Majorcan houses possess the same idea in the most understated, yet powerful, way.

Utzon's inventiveness in using locally sourced, humble materials is part of the magic of Can Lis and is consistent with all of his work, where a kit of parts, or the standard elements of an additive architecture, combine to make forms as diverse as a bench or a shell spanning the Opera House. The sandstone blocks, quarried in nearby Salinas, are common in that corner of Majorca and have been used for generations for building even the most humble of farm buildings and field walls, although the quarry is now depleted and shut down. The same stone

LEFT:
The court of Can Lis

OPPOSITE:
Interior view of the living room of Can Lis

was also once used to build the cathedral in Palma de Mallorca. This *marés* stone has a golden, buttery colour and a sandy texture, and was cut out of the quarry by a giant circular saw that first cut a chequerboard of incisions down into the bed; a horizontal cut then yielded the blocks like sugar cubes. The concentric circular saw-marks on the stone surface evoke the circular motifs of the Opera House shell drawings, give life to the inert material and hint that this may be a living thing, like a tree cut down with its grain revealed on the surface. A different, harder stone from a quarry in Santanyi some 6 km (4 miles) away, cut in the same sizes, was used for floor surfaces and this has a smoother, denser texture and a light grey colour that absorbs any reflected glare from the sun.

Beneath one colonnade of the open court, a stone and glazed tiled bench and dining table are built-in, as if fossilised. To the front, two steps drop towards the cliff edge with a low, stone wall and a single stone slab that lies like a segment of a fallen column, given use as a table by a glazed brown tiled surface. A small enigmatic court lies alongside the main courtyard, enclosed by high walls yet

opened up by semi-circular apertures (Utzon liked to describe the effect of the main semicircular cut-out and the horizon beyond as like a full wine glass). The court is empty save a stone-built, glazed tiled, semicircular table that suggests dining, but there are no seats, so with a single dark blue tile on the table's rim, this suddenly becomes a compass pointing due south. This is the full stop to the ensemble of buildings that make Can Lis and has a strange, temple-like, still atmosphere, with curved shadows that attempt to join up to form a circle on the floor and hint back to the crescent at the entrance. For Utzon, this idea comes directly from the traditional Danish farmhouse where an open garden space, a *vinterhave*, provides a place to sit and work with plants, so placed to admit the sun in winter but remain shaded in summer.

While the courtyard of Can Lis opens out to the sea, the living room seems to fold in and make an intense union of place and horizon. Entered from a shaded courtyard furnished with built-in seats and planters, through a four-bayed colonnade, the living room is essentially a cubic volume some 4.5 m sq (14 ft 9 in sq), but a single column with lintels above articulates this space, defining the route into the room. The surprise of entering a tall space combines with the even light without glare and an intense silence. The view through the different sized, deep bays is brought sharply into focus and the segments of a single horizon are the invitation to sit down on the semicircular seat to watch the drama that nature plays out. The plan, with the five deep, tapering windows like fingers stretching out to the ocean, has an uncanny similarity to Andrea Palladio's Teatro Olimpico in Vicenza, with its five diminishing openings focused onto the semicircular auditorium seats. Utzon related how the deep reveals of the palace at Versailles were an influence, whilst other references, from thick-walled vernacular buildings to the splayed openings in Corbusier's Ronchamp chapel, abound. These extraordinary stone eyes onto the ocean, however, really have no like, but are part of the inventiveness of an architect at the height of his powers. The fact that one can actually inhabit these funnels, like personal chapels off a nave, adds to their presence. This intensity is further enhanced by the fact that there is no window – no frames or shadows – only glass held in frames placed on the outside of the walls, influenced by the empty apertures of Sigurd Lewerentz's St Mark's Church in Björkhagen, completed two years earlier.

It is not just the deep bays that form the windowless windows, but the outer sheltering structure, a kind of loggia that provides shade that prevents glare from the glass, rendering it invisible. This outer architecture is reminiscent of Kahn 'wrapping ruins' around his buildings, a style that he developed initially in his project for an embassy in Luanda, Angola. Kahn wrote that,

> I am doing a building in Africa, which is very close to the equator. The glare is killing. Everybody looks black against the sunlight . . . So therefore I thought of the beauty of ruins . . . and so I thought of wrapping ruins around buildings: you might say encasing a building in a ruin so that you look through the wall which has its apertures as if by accident . . . I felt this would be an answer to the glare problem.

The twin phenomenon of the sea and the horizon being sucked into the room is magically balanced by the impression of being fired out simultaneously through the five apertures. Central to this drama is the not quite semicircular stone-built seat, furnished with dark blue tiles and crisp white linen cushions, that sits not quite square to the room but shifted to orient due south and is complemented by a segmented arc of table that was the family's auditorium to nature. High up on the west wall is a slit window, with the glass simply bonded to the outside wall as Utzon had so admired in Lewerentz's chapel at Klippan in Sweden, that lets the sun kiss the stone in a blaze of light just before evening each day. It is this small touch that makes the living room at Can Lis an absolutely unforgettable, timeless experience. Externally, the drama is hidden beneath the sheltering portico that shades the windows and lends a static, temple-like quality – even the slit that has such an impact internally is mute – only the twin Catalan triangular chimneys, so typical of Majorcan village houses, draw the eye.

CAN LIS, PORTO PETRO, MAJORCA

The journey from building to building continues from the shaded court at the back of the living block, across stepping stones and past a twisted tree to enter a further court, this one with no stone-built furniture, only planting and a single doorway into what becomes two bedrooms, paired around a central covered patio. Each is entered by a shared lobby with a small utilitarian bathroom and each is expressed as a separate volume with a pair of stone-eyed bay windows, miniature versions of those in the living room scaled to suit the reclining viewer in the built-in bed alcove, replete with cellular stone book recesses and fronted by a small glazed tiled table. These rooms find union in the central patio. Leaving the bedroom court, one last step across a small divide brings you through a doorway into the final covered patio, where the stone-built furniture reappears in blue and white diagonal glazed tiles. This leads into a small lobby, with a bathroom, and then into the last guest bedroom.

Throughout, door and shutter frames are visibly fixed to one face of the stone apertures and the doors themselves made in boards held in place by neat rows of exposed nail heads; the stone jambs are neatly carved out with elliptical incisions that allow space for the door handles and surprisingly bring to mind Michelangelo's handrail detail on the Laurentian library stairs.

A love of glazed tiles is quite particular to Utzon. The tiled domes and faceted vaults in Islamic architecture provided direct inspiration for the shells of the Opera House, but it was the idea of placing glazed and matt tiles together with the logic that only the matt tiles were to be cut that created the iridescence that helped make the Opera House so memorable. At Can Lis the entrance is marked by a stone-built, glazed tiled bench – white and dark blue coloured tiles. This welcoming gesture is typical of Islamic and Mediterranean traditional dwellings, where social life abounds, immediately outside the front door. These tiles are also used for the internal built-in furniture, but external benches within the courts use tan coloured tiles, with either dark blue or white edges or cut patterns.

It now seems hard to imagine why the Utzons should have left this house, yet with the passing of the years their other site, 'Paradise', high up the mountainside behind the coastline, called and in 1994 they moved to their new home, Can Feliz, leaving Can Lis to their now grown-up family. Can Lis must be the least-visited and known of all the great houses of the 20th century and, like Utzon himself, this withdrawal from the world has lent an enigmatic quality that merely increases the interest and notoriety of both.

MARIE SHORT HOUSE, KEMPSEY, NEW SOUTH WALES, AUSTRALIA

Glenn Murcutt, 1975

FOR THE AUSTRALIAN NATION, their dependence on British culture was to end with the Second World War and afterwards it became something of a ritual for young architects to seek experience in Europe or America. This was bolstered by an abundance of American journals such as the *Architectural Forum*, *The Architectural Record* and John Entenza's *Arts & Architecture* bringing the latest developments of the exiled masters from the Bauhaus, Frank Lloyd Wright and the Case Study Houses to Australia. When Glenn Murcutt was just 15, he came across Mies van der Rohe's Farnsworth House in the October 1951 edition of *Architectural Forum* that his father subscribed to, and his interest in architecture took hold.

His father, Arthur, had worked in New Guinea from 1919, earning a living from boat building, in plantation work and running a sawmill, even working alongside Errol Flynn long before Hollywood beckoned. Although Glenn Marcus Murcutt was born in London in 1936 while his Australian parents were visiting Europe, he was to spend his first five years in New Guinea, where his father had by then turned to gold prospecting. Arthur was a believer in the 'economy of survival' and an admirer of the American writer Henry David Thoreau's spartan philosophy. He was a near tyrannical father and made his sons follow a regime of strenuous exercise and music practice every day before and after school. Returning to Sydney in 1941 with a fortune from the gold rush, he became a developer-builder and produced many houses based on the articles he had seen in the magazines.

Murcutt began to study architecture in 1956 at the Sydney Technical College, and soon developed an interest in the work of the Californian architects, particularly Richard Neutra and Craig Ellwood, both of whom advanced the idea of sensitivity to place and climate. Upon graduating, Murcutt worked for a few local practices that were working in the vein of Frank Lloyd Wright and Alvar Aalto. In 1962, he moved temporarily to London and, just as young Australians do today, used this as a

BELOW:
Glenn Murcutt in front of Marie Short House in 2009

MARIE SHORT HOUSE, KEMPSEY, NEW SOUTH WALES, AUSTRALIA

staging post to travel extensively across Europe and Scandinavia. He was most impressed by Jørn Utzon's housing schemes in Denmark and Aalto's work in Finland, particularly in the way they wove architecture and landscape together. On his return to Sydney, he set up his own practice in 1969.

Murcutt's early works, which he combined with teaching at the University of Sydney, were a combination of domestic extension, renovation and new-build projects that all demonstrated his reliance on the Miesian language of open-plan structures, steel frames and floating decks. This perhaps culminated with the Laurie Short House in Terrey Hills, a suburb of Sydney, in 1974. This house is a single-storey glass and steel pavilion sitting on a platform of brick paviours and nested against the trees of the Ku-ring-gai Chase National Park, so prone to bush fires. The house is striking in that the steel frame is painted black, as Murcutt had seen charred tree trunks on his first site visit. Although Miesian in form, Murcutt's emerging concerns with passive climatic control began to appear, with a permanent 20 cm (8 in) deep pool over the roof that not only acts as fireproofing but increases thermal insulation as well as cooling air that is directed down through a sun-breaker formed of angled louvres set within the roof plane above a large veranda. With this house, architecture is clearly set upon nature, rather than within it, in an exchange between man and nature. While working on this house, the client's mother, Marie Short, engaged Murcutt to design a new house for her on a site in farming country some 500 km (300 miles) north of Sydney.

The site was an existing farm that incorporated some 260 hectares (640 acres) of grazing and woodland and Marie wanted a house for her own occupation. It sits outside the town of Kempsey that was founded on the banks of the Macleay River in the mid-19th century (and named after the Kempsey Valley in Worcestershire, England). Initially the town had prospered on logging and sawmills until the red cedar trees were largely depleted by the 1920s, when agriculture became the mainstay of the local economy. Sitting on a loop in the river at the top of the flood plain and some 5 km (3 miles) from the coast, the town regularly suffered severe flooding. Kempsey sits at the mid-north of New South Wales and has a subtropical climate, so rainfall can be sudden and dramatic, and humidity is high in the summer but tempered by cool sea breezes from the north-east. In contrast, cool westerly winds prevail during winter. In what was to be Murcutt's first building outside the suburbs of Sydney, he took his first cues from nature – the prevailing winds, the torrential rain, the need for solar shading – so placed the house at the far end of the floodplain grasslands below, on the edge of a gentle slope leading down to the existing farm buildings. The Marie Short House was to represent a turning point in Murcutt's architecture. It domesticated the Miesian model by subjecting it to site-specific context, climate and limited local building skills.

Murcutt had studied Aboriginal traditions and customs – the natives of Australia had only been granted Australian citizenship in the mid-1960s and had to wait until 1972 for their rights to repossess some of their ancestral lands under Gough Whitlam's government – and he was fascinated by the way the native peoples had learnt to live in such a harsh land and leave it seemingly untouched. He learnt that certain communities in Western Australia had a saying that 'one must touch this earth lightly' and this chimed with his own emerging philosophy. He sought to achieve a relationship and respect between architecture and landscape, between man and place. He was also aware of Harry Sowden's book *Australian Woolsheds*, published in 1972, that revealed the clarity and appropriateness of the pioneer's response to the Australian landscape. Built using imported and lightweight components such as iron frames and corrugated and galvanised steel sheets, these elements were easy to transport and were to create colonial bungalows with wide verandas, agricultural and industrial buildings across the land. In 1996, Murcutt was to write that:

> I'm very interested in buildings that adapt to changes in climatic conditions according to the seasons, buildings capable of responding to our physical and psychological needs in the way that clothing does. We don't turn on the air-conditioning as we walk through the streets in high summer. Instead, we change the character of the clothing by which we are protected. Layering and changeability: this is the key, the combination that is worked into most of my buildings. Occupying one of these buildings is like sailing a yacht; you modify and manipulate its form and skin according to seasonal conditions and natural elements, and work with these to maximize the performance of the building. This involvement with the building also assists in the care for it. I am concerned about the exploitation of the natural environment in order to modify the internal climate of buildings. Architects must confront the perennial issues of light, heat, and humidity control yet take responsibility for the method and the materials by which, and out of which, a building is made. The considerations, context, and the landscape are some of the factors that are constantly at work in my architecture.

MARIE SHORT HOUSE, KEMPSEY, NEW SOUTH WALES, AUSTRALIA

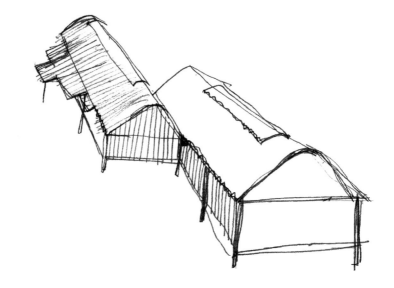

RIGHT:
Glenn Murcutt's sketch of Marie Short House

BELOW:
Plan of Marie Short House

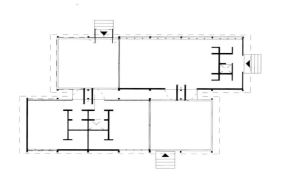

With the Marie Short House, Murcutt was able to bring together his concerns for both site specificity and climate, bringing together a light footprint on the land and the colonial traditional way of building for the first time.

At first glance, the house takes a beguilingly simple form of two parallel pavilions, each of six bays set side by side, with one pavilion slipped along from the other by the length of one bay. Each pavilion has a pitched galvanised sheet roof with a rounded apex above what reads as a framed structure. On plan, the northernmost wing provides living space and a master bedroom suite to one end, while the southernmost wing provides two additional bedrooms. Both bring Mies's Farnsworth House to mind, with all the service spaces – bathrooms, storage and kitchen – arranged as a closed 'box' floating within the open plan, as if giant pieces of furniture. The two volumes are joined together by a 1 m (3 ft 4 in) wide central 'gasket', a servant space, much as Kahn was fond of making. This space between the two wings provides a central low roof that acts as a gutter serving the pavilions either side.

209

TWENTY GREAT HOUSES OF THE TWENTIETH CENTURY

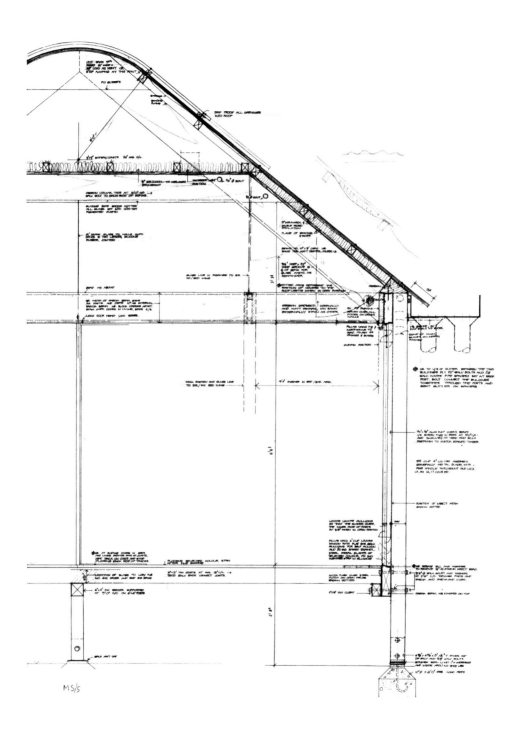

MARIE SHORT HOUSE, KEMPSEY, NEW SOUTH WALES, AUSTRALIA

OPPOSITE:
Glenn Murcutt's section drawing of Marie Short House

ABOVE:
Exterior view of Marie Short House

Each wing is formed of six structural bays, with the last two bays open beneath the roof. By arranging the wings side by side and 'handed', the side of each wing opens onto its adjoining terrace. This beguilingly simple plan arrangement breathes with the spirit of Mies – the Farnsworth House is inescapable – yet what makes the house unique is Murcutt's use of materials and roof form. No flat-roofed, steel-framed pavilion here, honed to the minimum, rather a sophisticated vernacular in wood and galvanised sheeting. The secret, as with all of Murcutt's work, lies in his beautifully drawn sections. These are

211

TOP:
Interior view of Marie Short House looking towards the living area

BOTTOM:
Interior view of Marie Short House looking from the living area towards the exterior

MARIE SHORT HOUSE, KEMPSEY, NEW SOUTH WALES, AUSTRALIA

working drawings, executed in a 0.1 mm Rapidograph pen and made to convey how the various parts go together. Replete with Murcutt's handwritten notes in architect's upper-case lettering, the sections concern themselves with bringing ordinary components together in a matter-of-fact way – to keep the rain out, provide daylight and ventilation, to keep floods and insects at bay, to shed rainwater, to keep the internal environment comfortable – it can all be seen in his consummate sectional drawings.

Murcutt chose to operate as a sole practitioner, so everything was drawn by him and this meant no compromise, no debate other than with his client. Years later, when he became celebrated and clients queued at his door, he simply remained on his own and clients joined a waiting list as he meticulously produced his buildings one by one.

The section drawings for the Marie Short house reveal an Oregon pine post and beam frame set at 3 m (12 ft) intervals. Set within this frame are modules of metal and glass louvres, four to each 3 m frame, together with insect screens and venetian blinds. The frame uprights are extended so that the floor lies 80 cm (24 ft) above the ground and connected with galvanised bolts to shoes that sit atop 30 cm (12 ft) diameter, 1.8 m (6 ft) deep piles set into the earth. The post and beam frame combine with cedar boarding to gables. The roof is galvanised corrugated metal sheeting fixed to timber battens over the frame, with 12 cm 'Insulwool' insulation sandwiched between the sheeting and timber internal lining. At the ridge, the sheets are bent using traditional methods and a continuous section along the ridge is lifted up to provide ventilation. At the eaves, the sheet roof oversails the walls without guttering to deal with flash flooding.

The palette of timber, glass and corrugated sheeting places the house squarely within the tradition of the Australian woolshed, while the rounded ridges to the pitched roofs recall traditional water tanks. With the pavilions lifted off the ground and featuring open verandas, early colonial homes are also brought to mind. At another level, it recalls the allegorical engraving of the Vitruvian primitive hut that was the frontispiece of the architectural theorist Marc-Antoine Laugier's *Essai sur l'architecture* in 1755, which was to become one of the most famous expressions of man's need for shelter in nature. With this house, Murcutt not only found his unique style but also created a contemporary expression for Australian domestic architecture.

Within the house, Mies's influence is subsumed by a Scandinavian atmosphere, with walls and ceilings faced in horizontal boards of hoop pine and floors of brush box timbers, complemented by Aalto furniture and light fittings. The timber interior lends a strong sense of warm domesticity and keeps cool while the heat outside the window is visible at every point. The outdoor terraces in eucalyptus wood also allow the inside–outside connection to blur.

Within five years, Marie Short decided that raising cattle did not suit her, so she put the house on the market. A friend called Murcutt to let him know his handiwork was for sale, so he quickly arranged a loan and bought the house in 1980. Murcutt was to enlarge the house substantially by adding three further bays to each wing, allowing each to operate separately for parents and children rather than the original night–day configuration. He also converted an old machine shed nearby into a guest studio. Like the Utzon house back in Denmark, you can have too much of a good thing and the Marie Short House, now also now known as the Murcutt House, lost its original sparse purity. Murcutt remains in the house with his second wife Wendy Lewin, also an architect and his only occasional collaborator.

The house set the template for all his later work and was hugely influential across Australia. Murcutt was awarded the Pritzker Prize in 2002, confirming his status as one of the leading architects in the world. He truly lived up to one of his favourite quotations by Henry David Thoreau: 'Since most of us spend our lives doing ordinary tasks, the most important thing is to carry them out extraordinarily well'.

Frontispiece from Marc-Antoine Laugier's *Essai sur l'architecture*, 1755

ACKNOWLEDGEMENTS

First and foremost, my thanks to my long-suffering 'architecture widow' Julie, who has not only endured my journey through practice, but has accompanied me on visits to most of the world's great buildings, including the houses in this book.

Growing up, my carpenter father's friendship with a local handyman and gardener, who turned out to be the architect Robert van't Hoff, had a profound and enduring influence on me. As I was good at drawing, Robert insisted that I must be an architect, long before I knew what the word meant. So, despite the tough times, I guess I should thank them both posthumously for my life's path.

Thank you to Jørn and Lis Utzon who allowed me, and my erudite friend Richard Weston, into their life during their last years. I think the monograph that Richard produced with the remarkable publisher Torsten Bløndal, and our subsequent books on the Utzon buildings, paid back their faith in us. It was a privilege to get to know Jørn and Lis, and touch genius.

Thank you, Brent Harris, not only for saving and renovating the extraordinary Desert House from the ravages of former owners of Neutra's masterpiece, but also for allowing Julie and me to visit and explore the house.

Chris Gray and Ross Couper drew the plans for this book, so thank you both.

I guess there are many people who have helped me along the way: Andrew Peckham, a great tutor at the then Polytechnic of Central London (PCL), who made me realise that writing is part of understanding architecture; Peter Phippen, who put great faith in my abilities as a newly qualified architect working with his firm of Phippen, Randall and Parkes; Colin Stansfield Smith, who also believed in me when I did not believe in myself (I miss you Colin); the amazing Isobel Allen, an architect and editor who put my own work on the cover of an architecture magazine and started a ball rolling; and my ever loyal friend, the most talented artist I have ever met, Helen Yardley, who was always there to keep me true to my vision when work was scarce.

Thank you to Val Rose at Lund Humphries who has been so enthusiastic and supportive in seeing this book fulfilled.

Finally, to my two wonderful grown-up kids, Izaak and MayBeth, who both announced to me (separately) that they were never going to do what I do, as I worked all the time. I was only drawing!

SELECT BIBLIOGRAPHY

While not an exhaustive selection, the following books have been of great help:

SCHRÖDER HOUSE

Baroni, D., *Gerrit Thomas Rietveld Furniture*, Academy Editions, London, 1978.

Küper, M., and van Zijl, I., *Gerrit Th. Rietveld: The Complete Works*, Princeton Architectural Press, Princeton, NJ, 1992.

van Zijl, I., *Gerrit Rietveld*, Phaidon Press, New York, 2010.

VILLA SAVOYE

Curtis, W., *Le Corbusier: Ideas and Forms*, Phaidon Press, London, 1986.

Ferleger Brades, S., Walker, M., Raeburn, M., and Wilson, V., *Le Corbusier: Architect of the Century*, Arts Council of Great Britain, London, 1987.

VILLA MÜLLER

Loos, C., *Adolf Loos: A Private Portrait*, Dopplehouse Press, Los Angeles, CA, 2011.

Gravagnuolo, B., *Adolf Loos: Theory and Works*, Idea Books Edizioni, Milan, 1982.

Masheck, J., *Adolf Loos: The Art of Architecture*, I.B. Tauris, New York, 2013.

Risselada, M. (ed.), *Raumplan versus Plan Libre*, Rizzoli, New York, 1988.

TUGENDHAT HOUSE

Hammer-Tugendhat, D., Hammer, I., and Tegethoff, W., *Tugendhat House*, Birkhäuser, Basel, 2015.

DALSACE HOUSE (MAISON DE VERRE)

Brace Taylor, B., *Pierre Chareau*, Taschen, Köln, 1998.

Futagawa, Y. (ed.), *La Maison de Verre*, A.D.A. Edita, Tokyo, 1988.

FALLINGWATER

Hess, A., and Weintraub, A., *Frank Lloyd Wright: The Houses*, Rizzoli, New York, 2005.

Hoffmann, D., *Fallingwater: The House and its History*, Dover Publications, New York, 1978.

McCarter, R., *Fallingwater*, Phaidon, London, 1994.

Toker, F., *Fallingwater Rising*, Alfred A. Knopf, New York, 2004.

VILLA BIANCA

Eisenman, P., *Giuseppe Terragni: Transformations, Decompositions, Critiques*, Monacelli, New York, 2003.

Marcianò, A.F., *Giuseppe Terragni: opera completa 1925–1945*, Officina Edizioni, Rome, 1987.

Schumacher, T., *Surface and Symbol: Giuseppe Terragni and the Architecture of Italian Rationalism*, Ernst & Sohn, Berlin, 1991.

Terragni, A., Libeskind, D., and Rosselli, P., *The Terragni Atlas*, National Committee for the Celebration of the Anniversary of the Birth of Giuseppe Terragni, Skira, Milan, 2004.

VILLA MAIREA

Stewart, J., *Alvar Aalto: Architect*, Merrell, London, 2017.

Weston, R., *Villa Mairea*, Phaidon, London, 1992.

Yoshida, N. (ed.), *Alvar Aalto Houses*, Architecture and Urbanism, A+U Publishing, Tokyo, 1998.

THE DESERT HOUSE

Boesiger, W., *Richard Neutra, 1923–50*, Verlag für Architecture, Zürich, 1966.

Drexler, A, and Hines, T., *The Architecture of Richard Neutra:*

TWENTY GREAT HOUSES OF THE TWENTIETH CENTURY

From International Style to Californian Modern, MOMA, New York, 1982.

Hines, T., *Richard Neutra and the Search for Modern Architecture*, Oxford University Press, Oxford, 1982.

EAMES HOUSE

Demetrios, E., *Eames: Beautiful Details*, Ammo, Los Angeles, CA, 2012.

Ince, C., and Johnson, L., *The World of Charles and Ray Eames*, Thames & Hudson, London, 2015.

FARNSWORTH HOUSE

Blaser, W., *West Meets East: Mies van der Rohe*, Birkhäuser, Basel, 1996.

Lohan, D., *Farnsworth House: Detail*, A.D.A. Edita, Tokyo, 1976.

Vandenberg, M., *Farnsworth House*, Phaidon, London, 2003.

UTZON HOUSE

Frampton, K., 'Jørn Utzon: Transcultural Form and the Tectonic Metaphor', in Frampton, K., and Cava, J., *Studies in Tectonic Culture*, MIT Press, Cambridge, MA, 1995.

Giedion, S., 'Jørn Utzon and the Third Generation', *Zodiac*, no.14, 1965.

Sheridan, M., *Landmarks: The Modern House in Denmark*, Hatje Cantz, Ostfildern, 2014.

Weston, R., *Utzon: Inspiration, Vision, Architecture*, Editions Bløndal, Hellerup, 2002.

NIEMEYER HOUSE (CASA DAS CANOAS)

Niemeyer, O., *The Curves of Time: The Memoires of Oscar Niemeyer*, Phaidon, London, 2000.

Underwood, D., *Oscar Niemeyer and Brazilian Free-Form Modernism*, George Braziller, New York, 1994.

MAISONS JAOUL

Benton, C., *Le Corbusier and the Maisons Jaoul*, Princeton Architectural Press, Princeton, NJ, 2009.

STAHL HOUSE (CASE STUDY HOUSE 22)

Smith, E., *Case Study Houses*, Taschen, Köln, 2002.

Steele, J., and Jenkins, D., *Pierre Koenig*, Phaidon, London, 1998.

GWATHMEY HOUSE

Arnell, P., and Bickford, T. (eds), *Charles Gwathmey and Robert Siegel: Buildings and Projects 1964–1984*, Harper & Row, London, 1984.

Collins, B., *Gwathmey Siegel Houses*, Monacelli, New York, 2000.

FISHER HOUSE

Brownlee, D., and De Long, D., *Louis I. Kahn: In the Realm of Architecture*, Rizzoli, New York, 1992.

Gast, K., *Louis I. Kahn: The Idea of Order*, Birkhäuser, Basel, 1998.

McCarter, R., *Louis I. Kahn*, Phaidon, London, 2005.

Marcus, G., and Whitaker, W., *The Houses of Louis Kahn*, Yale University Press, New Haven, CT, 2103.

Tyng, A., *Beginnings: Louis I. Kahn's Philosophy of Architecture*, John Wiley, New York, 1984.

Wurman, S., *What Will Be Has Always Been: The Words of Louis I. Kahn*, Rizzoli, New York, 1986.

SAN CRISTÓBAL

Ambasz, E., *The Architecture of Luis Barragán*, MOMA, New York, 1976.

Júlbez, J., Palomar, J., and Eguiarte, G., *The Life and Work of Luis Barragán*, Rizzoli, New York, 1997.

Futagawa, Y. (ed.), *Luis Barragán*, A.D.A. Edita, Tokyo, 1979.

CAN LIS

Pardey, J., *Utzon: Two Houses on Majorca*, Editions Bløndal, Hellerup, 2004.

Weston, R., *Utzon: Inspiration, Vision, Architecture*, Editions Bløndal, Hellerup, 2002.

MARIE SHORT HOUSE

Fromonot, F., *Glenn Murcutt: Buildings & Projects 1962–2003*, Thames & Hudson, New York, 2003.

Gusheh, M., *Glenn Murcutt: Thinking Drawing, Working Drawing*, Toto Publishing, Tokyo, 2015.

IMAGE CREDITS

© ADAGP, Paris and DACS, London / © FLC / ADAGP, Paris and DACS, London 2020: 25 (photo © Hans Jan Dürr), 27, 28, 29, 30, 32, 33, 34, 35 (photo © Montse Zamorano); © Alvar Aalto Foundation: 85, 86, 87, 90, 93; © APA Picturedesk: 39, 40; Courtesy Architecture Foundation Australia: 209, 210; © ARS, NY and DACS, London 2020: 68, 72 (photo © Montse Zamorano), 75 (photo © Montse Zamorano); © ARS, NY and DACS, London 2020. Photo Courtesy of the Western Pennsylvania Conservancy: 10, 68, 73; © Vasily Babourov: 80; © Barragan Foundation / DACS 2020. Courtesy Barragan Foundation, Switzerland, photo Ursula Bernath: 185; © Barragan Foundation/DACS 2020: 186, 189; Werner Blaser: 118; bpk / Kunstbibliothek, SMB, photothek Willy Römer / Willy Römer: 48; Bill Brookover: 180; © Anthony Browell, courtesy Architecture Foundation Australia: 205, 206, 211, 212 (both); City Museum of Prague, photo by Pavel Štecha: 44; © Collection Centraal Museum, Utrecht: 19, 21; © DACS 2020: 20; © DACS 2020. Photograph: Miloš Budík: 55; © DACS 2020, courtesy Canadian Centre for Architecture. Photograph by Kurt Schwitters; © DACS 2020. Collection Centraal Museum, Utrecht: 20; © DACS 2020. Photo © Hans Jan Dürr: 22; © DACS 2020, courtesy Library of Congress, Prints & Photographs Division, HABS. Photograph by Jack E. Boucher: 116; © DACS 2020, courtesy Library of Congress, Prints & Photographs Division, photograph by Carol M. Highsmith: 121; © DACS 2020. Photo by Rudolf Sandalo Jr, 1931, Brno City Museum: 47, 49, 51; © DACS 2020. Photo by Andrew Sides (waterboyzoo on flickr): 22; © DACS 2020. Photo © Montse Zamorano: 123; © DACS 2020. Photograph by David Židlický: 53, 54; © Detre Library and Archives, Sen. John Heinz History Centre: 69; © Eames Office, LLC (eamesoffice.com): 109, 110, 111; Courtesy Editions Blondal: 126, 129, 130, 132, 133; © F.L.C /ADAGP, Paris and DACS, London 2020: 145 (Photo Lucien Hervé), 146, 149 (photo SEIER+SEIER), 150, 151, 152; © Joe Fletcher: 101; © Scott Frances/OTTO: 165, 158, 170; © J. Paul Getty Trust. Getty Research Institute, Los Angeles: 2, 6, 97, 100, 103, 104, 106, 107, 113, 155, 156, 158, 162, 163; Courtesy Daniela Hammer-Tugendhat: 48; © John Pardey Architects: 19, 23, 31, 43, 52, 64, 70, 71, 81, 82, 89, 102, 112, 119, 120, 131, 142, 148, 161, 169, 175, 177, 178, 183, 184, 188, 196, 197, 209; © Library of Congress, Prints & Photographs Division. Photo by Al Ravenna: 69; © MAD, Paris: 58; © Mark Lyon: 57, 60; Esther McCoy papers, 1876-1990, Archives of American Art, Smithsonian Institution: 99; Norman McGareth: 166; Museum of Decorative Arts in Prague: 37; © Niemeyer, Oscar / DACS 2020: 137 (photo © Julian Weyer), 138, 140, 141 (photo Rüediger Müller), 143; Courtesy Northwestern Memorial Hospital: 119; RIBA Collections: 215; Bent Ryberg/www.edition-blondal.dk: 193, 195, 196, 197, 198, 199, 200; Leslie Schwartz, © 2013 Eames Office LLC: 114; Courtesy of the Department of Special Collections, Stanford University Libraries: 87; Mark Trueman: 90; © Utzon Centre: 128, 134 (both), 135, 194, 201; Photo © Ezio Zupelli: 77, 82.

INDEX

Page numbers in *italics* refer to illustrations/captions.

901 Washington Boulevard 109, 115
Aalto, Alvar 14, 84–95, *86*, *87*, *91*, 129, 206, 213
Adler and Sullivan 69
Ahlberg, Hakon 129
Ahlström, Walter 88, 89, 94, 95
Alessi 171
American Academy, Rome 176
Ammann, Gustav 103
Ando, Tapado 14
Après le cubisme 29
Architectural Forum 206
Architectural Record 99, 206
Armour Institute, Chicago 54
Aronoff family 170
Artek 88, 95
Arts & Architecture 108, 110–111, 156–7, 159, 206
Asilo Infantile Sant'Elia school, Como 81
Asplund, Erik Gunnar 86, 129

Bac, Ferdinand 184
Bagsværd Church 199
Bailey House, Los Angeles 157, *158*, 159, 162
Baker, Josephine 35
Baldo, Annita 140, 143
Barragán, Luis 8, 14, 182–91, *185*
Bauhaus 38, 49, 69, 122, 169, 206

Bayview, Sydney 194, 195, 196
Beauvallon, St Tropez 59–60
Beaux-Arts teaching system 138, 176
Beck, Claire 39–41
Behrens, Peter 28, 48
Benjamin, Walter 65
Bijvoet, Bernard 59
Borges, Jorge Luis 187
Braque, Georges 35
Brazilian Communist Party 142
Brazilian Pavilion, 1939 World Fair 139
Bucher, Lothar 174
Burle Marx, Roberto 141–2

Californian Modernism 156
Calvinism 18, 21
Can Lis, Porto Petro 192–203, *193*, *195*, *196*, *197*, *198*, *199*, *200*, *201*
Carpenter, Marion 118
Casa del Fascio, Como 79, *79*, 80
Casa Giuliani Frigerio, Como 80, *80*
Case Study House Program 110–111, 157, 160, 163, 206
Castro, Fidel 142
Chandigarh 146, 148
Chareau, Pierre 14, 15, 56–65, *59*, 92
'Chicago School' 69, 100, 120–21
Cité de Refuge, Paris 35
Cocteau, Jean 65
Cody, William 105
Committee of Architects for the Study of the Environment (CASE) 169
Correa, Charles 153

Costa, Lúcio 138–9
Country House plan 51, 72, 101, *119*, 119, 133, 171, 188
Crystal Palace, London 7, 58, 61, 174
Cubism 29, 35, 51, 166

Dalbet, Louis 63
Dalsace House (Maison de Verre), Paris 15, 56–65, *57*, *58*, *60*, *61*, *63*, *64*, 92
Dalsace, Annie 60, 62, 65
Dalsace, Jean 60, 61, 65
Dante (Alighieri) 82
Danteum, Rome 82–3, *82*
de Chirico, Giorgio 185, 188
De Stijl 13, 18, 19, 21, 23, 24, 51, 63, 69, 72, 80, 170, 185, 188
Desert House, Palm Springs 15, 96–105, *96–7*, *101*, *102*, *103*, *104*, 111, 113
'Desk MB673' 63
Deutscher Werkbund 38, 48, 49, 61
Dom-ino system 23, 28–9, *30*, 121
Dominican Motherhouse 177
Doshi, B.V. 153
Dubuffet, Jean 147
Duiker, Jan 60, 87, 142
Dyte, Louise (Dollie) 59, 60

Eames House, Pacific Palisades 6, 106–115, *107*, *112*, *113*, *114*, 157, 162
Eames, Charles and Ray 6, 8, 14, 15, 106–115, *107*, *109*, *110*, *111*

INDEX

Egerstrom, Folke 184, 190
Einstein, Albert 70, 166
Eisenman, Peter 80, 83, 166, 170, 171
Eisler brothers 50
Eliot, T.S. 95
Ellwood, Craig 157, 160, 206
Entenza, John 108, 110–111, 114, 206
Entwistle, Clive 148
Essai sur l'architecture 213, *215*
Essex Falls, New Jersey 169

Fagus Factory, Alfeld 61
Fallingwater, Bear Run 10, 11, 66–75, *66–7, 68, 70, 71, 72, 73, 75,* 89, 98, 101, 140, 149, 157, 161, 177, 194
Farnsworth House, Fox River 58, 116–125, *116–117, 120, 121, 123,* 142, 152, 159, 206, 209, 211
Farnsworth, Edith 118–119, *119,* 121, 122–3, 124, 125
Fehn, Sverre 14
Fine Arts Academy, Rio de Janeiro 135
Finnish Pavilion, 1937 World Fair 88
First World War 21, 28, 30, 59, 86, 138
Fisher House, Hatboro 172–81, *173, 177, 178, 179, 180*
Fisher, Norman and Doris 176, 177, 178, *179*
Five Architects 166, 169, 171
'Five Points' 15, 28
Foster, Norman 65, 157
Freud, Ernst 98
Freud, Sigmund 98
Fuentes, Carlos 191
Fueter, Rudolph 148

Gale House, Chicago 71
Gallis, Yvonne 34, *35,* 35, 146
Gaudí, Antoni 187
Gehry, Frank 14
German Pavilion, Barcelona 53, *54,* 133
Giedion, Sigfried 93
Glass Pavilion, Cologne 61
Goebbels, Joseph 49
Golden Ratio 78, 80, 82

Goldman and Salatsch 38
Graves, Michael 166, 171
Gropius, Walter 28, 48, 61, 146
Grundtvig Church, Copenhagen *129, 129*
Gullichsen, Harry 88, 89, 94
Gullichsen, Maire 88, 89, 90, 91, 92
Gwathmey House, Amagansett 13, 164–71, *165, 167, 168, 169, 170*
Gwathmey, Charles 13, 102, 164–71, *166*
Gwathmey, Robert and Rosalie 166

Hadid, Zaha 14
Hahl, Nils-Gustav 88, 95
Hammer-Tugendhat, Daniela 55
Hammer, Ivo 55
Harris, Brent and Beth 105
Hedquist, Paul 129
Hedrich, Bill 68, 157
Hejduk, John 166, 170–71
Henny, A.B. 18
Herzog and de Meuron 14
Hilberseimer, Ludwig 49
Hilversum Town Hall, Rotterdam 87
Hitchcock, Henry Russell 99
Hitler, Adolf 49, 94
Hladká, Karla 55
Hoffmann, Josef 12
House 10 171
House Beautiful 122
House Van den Doel, Ilpendam 24, *25*
House X 170
Howe, Jack *68,* 68
Huset i Haven (Ønskehuset) *133,* 133
Huszár, Vilmos 19

Illinois Institute of Technology 54, 118
Imperial Hotel, Tokyo 69, 73
Imperial Institute of Technology 98
Indian Institute of Management, Ahmedabad 177
International Style 14, 15, 69, 70, 73, 82, 87, 92, 101, 102, 122, 138, 185

Jaoul, André 146–7, 148, 152

Jaoul, Marie 150
Jaoul, Michel 146, 150
Jaoul, Suzanne 152
Japanese style 14, 23, 61, 74, 75, 91, 92, 102, 112, 132, 133, 141, 159
Jardinette Apartments, Hollywood 99
Jeanneret, Pierre 146
Jensen-Klint, Peder *129,* 129
Johnson, Philip 125, 169

Kahn, Louis 14, 15, 44, 53, 83, 151, 166, 172–81, *174,* 197, 202, 209
Kahn, Nathaniel 177
Kandinsky, Wassily 49
Kapsa and Müller 42
Kaufmann, Edgar 9, 69, *69,* 70, 72, 74, 75, 98, 100, 102, 104, 105
Kaufmann, Edgar Jnr 70
Kaufmann, Liliane 70, 72, 104, *105,* 105
Kentucky Knob, Pennsylvania 152
Klaarhamer, P.J.C. 18
Klee, Paul 171
Klint, Kaare 129–30
Koenig, Pierre 14, 154–63, *157, 158*
Kok, Antony 19
Kokoschka, Oskar 38
Korman House 181
Kröller-Müller Museum, Otterlo 22, 24

L'Esprit nouveau 30, 41
La Sainte-Baume hotel 147
La Ville Radieuse 147
Las Arboledas, Mexico City 187–9
Lasdun, Denys 153
Laugier, Marc-Antoine 213, *215*
Laurie Short House, Terrey Hills 207
Lautner, John 142
Le Corbusier 13, 14, 15, 23, 26–35, *29, 30, 35,* 41, 48, 52, 65, 69, 78, 81, 83, 87, 88, 89, 121, 124, 138–9, 142, 144–53, *146, 152,* 166, 169, 174, 184, 187, 202
Lebensreform movement 30
Lewerentz, Sigurd 202
Lewin, Wendy 214

221

Lingeri, Pietro 82, 83
Lohan, Dirk 125
Loos, Adolf 12, 13, 36–45, *39*, *40*, 48, 52, 64, 185
Los Clubes 189–90
Lössl, Gustav 55
Louisiana Museum of Modern Art 133
Lovell Beach House, Newport 73, 99
Lovell Health House, Los Angeles 73, 99–100, *100*
Lovell, Philip 99, 100
Lovell, Leah 99
Luanda embassy 202

Mackintosh, Charles Rennie 59
Magid, Jill 191
Magritte, René 188
Maison Citrohan 23
Maison d'Artiste 147
Maison Monol 147
Maisons Jaoul, Paris 144–53, *144–5*, *148*, *149*, *150*, *151*
Mäkiniemi, Elsa 95
Malraux, André 34
Manilow, Barry 105
Marie Short House, Kempsey 14, 204–14, *205*, *209*, *210*, *211*, *212*
Markelius, Sven 86
Markelius, Viola 95
Marmol, Leo 105
Marquez, Gabriel Garcia 41
Marsh, 'Red' 104
Marsio, Aino 86, *87*, 89, 95
Marx, Lora 119
Massachusetts Institute of Technology 94
Maternová, Eva 45
Matisse, Henri 189
Mawer, Simon 50
McCormick House, Elmhurst 125
Meier, Richard 13, 166, 169–70, 171
Messerschmitt, Willy 55
MGM Studios 108
Milan Polytechnic 78
Miller, Herman 110

Miller, J.H. 99
Ministry of Education and Health, Brazil 139, 141
Miró, Joan 65
Modern Movement 53, 69, 139
Moller House, Vienna 12
Monastery of La Tourette 146
Mondrian, Piet 19
Mulder, Bertus 25
Müller House, Prague 12
Müller, František 42, 43, 45
Müllerova, Milada 42, 45
Murcutt, Arthur 206
Murcutt, Glenn 8, 14, 204–214, *206*, *209*, *210*
Museum of Modern Art, New York 70, 108, 122, 169, 184
Musil, Robert 42
Mussolini 78, 79, 82, 170
Muthesius, Hermann 59

National Assembly Building of Bangladesh, Dhaka 177
National Fascist Party 79, 170
Neoplasticism 19
Neutra, Richard 14, 15, 73, 96–105, 99, 108, 111, 113, 157, 206
Neutra, Samuel and Elizabeth 98
New National Gallery, Berlin 53
New York Five (the Whites) 14, 80, 83, 169
Niedermann, Dione 98, 99, 99
Niemeyer House (Casa das Canoas), Rio de Janeiro 136–143, *136–7*, *138*, *140*, *141*, *142*, *143*
Niemeyer, Oscar 8, 14, 136–43, *138*, *140*
Novocomum, Como 78

OMA/Rem Koolhaus 14
Ornament and Crime 38, *40*, 40, 41, 43
Oud, Jacobus 87
Ozenfant, Amédéé 29, 41

Paimio sanatorium *87*, 87–8
Palais Stoclet 12

Palladio, Andrea 13, 30, 201
Palumbo, Lord Peter 125, 152
Pavillon Suisse, Paris 35, 139
Paxton, Joseph 174
Paz, Octavio 187
Perret, Auguste 28, 147
Perriand, Charlotte 52
Petite Maison de Weekend, Paris 147
Picasso, Pablo 13, 15, 35, 65, 102, 147, 166
Plyformed Wood Company 109
Porush, William 159
Propos d'urbanisme 148
Purism 30, 151

Quattro libri dell'architecttura 13, 30

Radice, Mario 83
Radziner, Ron 105
Raumplan 12, 13, 42, 44, 45
Red-Blue Chair 19, *20*, 21, 22
Reich, Lilly *52*, 52, 54, 119
Rietveld, Gerrit 13, 15, 16–25, *19*, *21*, *22*, *25*, 63, *112*
Rietveld, Johannes 18
Robie House 12
Rogers, Richard 65
Ronchamp chapel 142, 146, 166, 202
Roq et Rob hotel 147
Rossi, Aldo 42
Royal Academy of Fine Arts, Copenhagen 129
Royal Academy School of Architecture, Copenhagen 129–30
Rubin, Robert 65
Rudolph, Paul 153, 169
Rufer House, Vienna 42

Saarinen, Eero 108, *110*, 111
Salk Institute, California 197
San Cristóbal, Mexico City 182–91, *182–3*, *184*, *186*, *188*, *189*
Sarabhai, Manorama 152
Savoye, Emilie 13, 31, 33, 34
Savoye, Pierre 13, 31, 34

INDEX

Savoye, Roger 34
Schindler, Rudolph 73, 98–9, *99*, 100
Schinkel, Karl Friedrich 48, 49
Schoberth, Louis 55
Schoenberg, Arnold 38
Schönbrunn Palace, Vienna 103
School of Architecture, Helsinki 86
Schoon 21
Schröder House, Utrecht, Netherlands 16–25, *16–17, 20, 22, 23*, 112
Schröder-Schräder, Truus 18, *21*, 21–2, 23, 24–5
Scully, Vincent 171
Secession 12, 38
Second World War 13, 34, 78, 79, 82, 104, 147, 206
Seidler, Harry 142
Seurat, Georges 166
Shulman, Julius 104, *109*, 113, 156, *156*, 157, 160, 162
Siegel, Robert 169
Siza, Álvaro 14
Skønvirke 129
Smith House, Darien 13, 169
Soriano, Raphael 157
Sowden, Harry 208
Speer, Albert 49
Spence, Basil 153
Stahl House, (Case Study House 22) Los Angeles *2*, 154–63, *155, 156, 159, 161, 162, 163*
Stahl, Buck 160, 162
State Loan Programme 128
Steiner House, Vienna 12, 38, 42
Stirling, James 153
Sullivan, Louis 69, 99, 100
Sydney Opera House 128, 131, 135, 194, 195, 199, 200, 203
Sydney Technical College 206

Tanguy, Yves 65
Taut, Bruno 61
Teatro Olimpico, Vicenza 201
Teige, Karel 54
Terragni, Attilio 78

Terragni, Giuseppe 14, 24, 76–83, *78, 79, 80, 82*, 170
Thoreau, Henry David 206, 214
Trenton Bath House 44, 174–5, *175*
Tugendhat House, Brno 45, 46–55, *46–7, 49, 51, 52, 53, 54, 55*, 119, 140
Tugendhat, Fritz and Grete *48*, 48, 49, 54, 55
Tula House 14

UNESCO World Heritage Sites 25, 55, 191
Unité d'Habitation, Marseilles 146
Unity Temple, Chicago 69, 71
University of Chicago 118
University of Philadelphia 176
University of Southern California 158, 163
University of Sydney 207
Utrecht Museum of Applied Arts 18
Utzon House, Hellebæk 126–35, *126–7, 131, 132, 134, 135*, 214
Utzon-Frank, Einar 129
Utzon, Aage 129
Utzon, Jørn 8, 14, 126–35, *128, 130, 135*, 192–203, *194*, 207
Utzon, Lin 132, 135
Utzon, Lis (née Fenger) 129, 135, 194, 195

van der Leck, Bart 19
van der Rohe, Mies 7, 9, 13, 14, 24, 28, 45, 46–55, *48, 54*, 58, 72, 101, 116–125, *118, 119*, 133, 140, 142, 146, 152, 159, 171, 188, 206, 207, 208, 209, 211, 213
van Doesburg, Theo 19
van't Hoff, Robert 18, *19*, 19, 69, 98
Vantongerloo, Georges 19
Verloop, J.N. 18
Vers une architecture 13, 30, 138
Viljo, Eeva 95
Villa Bianca, Seveso 76–83, *77, 81, 82, 83*
Villa Henny, Utrecht 18, *19*, 69

Villa La Roche, Paris 87, 166
Villa Mairea, Noormarkku 84–95, *84–5, 89, 90, 91, 93, 94*
Villa Müller, Prague 12, 36–45, *37, 38, 43, 44*
Villa Perls, Berlin 48
Villa Sarabhai, Ahmedabad 152–3
Villa Savoye, Poissy 13, 26–35, *27, 28, 31, 32, 33, 34*, 65, 124, 147, 153, 187
Villa Stein, Garches 87
Voysey, C.F.A. 59

Wagner, Otto 39
Walker, Rodney 111
Waring and Gillow 59
Wechsler, Judith 115
Wils, Jan 19
Wittgenstein, Ludwig 12, 38
Wohlert, Wilhelm *133*, 133
Wolf House 50
Wright, Frank Lloyd 12, 13, 14, 18, 66–75, *69*, 89, 98–9, 100, 101–102, *105*, 105, 122, 124, 129, 130, 131, 133, 140, 149, 152, 161, 177, 194, 206

Zevi, Bruno 83
Zonnestraal Sanatorium, Hilversum 59–60, 87, 142

First published in 2020 by Lund Humphries

Lund Humphries
Office 3, Book House
261A City Road
London EC1V 1JX
UK
www.lundhumphries.com

20/20: Twenty Great Houses of the Twentieth Century © John Pardey, 2020
All rights reserved

ISBN: 978-1-84822-353-0

A Cataloguing-in-Publication record for this book is available from the British Library

All rights reserved. No part of this publication may be reproduced, stored in a retrieval system or transmitted in any form or by any means, electrical, mechanical or otherwise, without first seeking the permission of the copyright owners and publishers. Every effort has been made to seek permission to reproduce the images in this book. Any omissions are entirely unintentional, and details should be addressed to the publishers.

John Pardey has asserted his right under the Copyright, Designs and Patent Act, 1988, to be identified as the Author of this Work.

Designed by Adrian Hunt and Crow Books

Set in Mont and Arnhem

Printed in China

Front cover: Interior of The Desert House, designed by Richard Neutra in 1946.
Image © J. Paul Getty Trust, Getty Research Institute, Los Angeles.
Page 2: Exterior view of Stahl House, designed by Pierre Koenig in 1960.
Image © J. Paul Getty Trust, Getty Research Institute, Los Angeles.
Page 6: Charles and Ray Eames in the living room of Eames House in 1958. Photograph by Julius Shulman. Image © J. Paul Getty Trust, Getty Research Institute, Los Angeles.